Types of Funeral Services and Ceremonies
2nd Edition

Content Written & Owned by:

National Association
of
Colleges
of
Mortuary Science

Published by:

Funeral Service Education Resource Center

FSERC

Dedicated to the Advancement of Funeral Service Education

Copyright © 2016 by Funeral Service Education Resource Center and National Association of Colleges of Mortuary Science, Inc.

All rights reserved. No part of this publication may be reproduced, distributed, or transmitted in any form or by any means, including photocopying, recording, or other electronic or mechanical methods, without the prior written permission of the publisher, except in the case of brief quotations embodied in critical reviews and certain other noncommercial uses permitted by copyright law. For permission requests, write to the publisher, addressed "Attention: Permissions Coordinator," at the address below.

Funeral Service Education Resource Center
12316A North May Avenue, Suite #209
Oklahoma City, OK 73120

2nd Edition 2015, Printed in the U.S.A.

ISBN: 978-0-692-67590-8

Published by The:
Funeral Service Education Resource Center
12316-A North May Avenue, Suite #209
Oklahoma City, Oklahoma 73120
Phone: 405-226-3155
Email: fnrleducation@gmail.com
Website: www.fserc.com

Foreword to the Second Edition

The National Association of Colleges of Mortuary Science, Inc. recently recognized a need to re-address the previous edition of the Types of Funeral Services and Ceremonies text. This revision was designed to enhance the previous body of work, and provide a more useful tool for the funeral service profession.

Enhancements to the text include:
- Basic Objectives for the Funeral Service Profession, as defined by the American Board of Funeral Service Education, have been added to the text.
- Over 50 photographs have been inserted throughout the text.
- Visuals aids, diagrams, and timelines have been included to provide instructors, students, and funeral service professionals with a better understanding of faith development and faith practices.
- Discussion boxes have been utilized to clarify certain topics and provide talking points throughout the chapters.
- "Helpful Terms" appear in each chapter, along with comprehensive glossaries at the end of each section.
- "In a Nutshell" summaries have been provided to assist students and professionals to develop a mental picture of the funeral practices of each group discussed.
- Finally, each chapter concludes with a list of suggested Study Questions which focus on key terminology and concepts addressed within that chapter.

The goal of The National Association of Colleges of Mortuary Science, Inc. is that this text will be an informative and enjoyable tool to utilize. Appreciation is expressed to all who partook in the development, review, and editing process.

Reproduction of this material is expressly forbidden except where permission is granted by the National Association of Colleges of Mortuary Science, Inc., and the Funeral Service Education Resource Center.

Acknowledgements

"The National Association of Colleges of Mortuary Science would like to thank iStock by Getty Images for the photographs utilized in the second edition of *Types of Funeral Services and Ceremonies*."

"The National Association of Colleges of Mortuary Science would like to thank Brian C. Mullins for development of the visual aids and charts."

Table of Contents

Chapter 1 The Protestant Funeral Rite – Liturgical 1

    The Episcopal Funeral Rite 11

    The Lutheran Funeral Rite... 16

    Glossary of Liturgical Protestant Terms 22

    Chapter 1 Review 24

Chapter 2 The Protestant Funeral Rite – Non-Liturgical 25

    The Swiss Brethren Traditions: Mennonite and Amish Funeral Rites 32

        The Mennonite Tradition 33

        The Amish Tradition 36

    Glossary Chapter Two 39

    Chapter 2 Review 40

Chapter 3 The Restoration Funeral Rite – Non-Liturgical 41

        The Church of Christ, Scientist Christian Science.. 43

        The Mormon Funeral Rite (LDS and RLDS) 46

        The Jehovah's Witness Funeral Rite 51

    Glossary Chapter Three 53

    Chapter 3 Review 54

Chapter 4 The Roman Catholic Funeral Rite 55

    Glossary of Roman Catholic Terms... 69

    Other, Related Terms 73

    Chapter 4 Review 76

Chapter 5 The Eastern Orthodox Funeral Rite 77

    Glossary of Orthodox Terms 87

    Chapter 5 Review 88

Chapter 6 The Jewish Funeral Rite 89

    The Orthodox Jewish Funeral Rite.. 91

    The Conservative and Reformed Jewish Funeral Rite 99

    Glossary of Jewish Terms 100

    Other, Related Terms 102

    Chapter 6 Review 104

Chapter 7 The Islamic Funeral Rite...105

    Glossary of Islamic Terms 112

    Chapter 7 Review 113

Chapter 8 The Buddhist Funeral Rite...114

    The Japanese Buddhist Funeral Rite..121

    The Buddhist Glossary 127

    Chapter 8 Review 128

Chapter 9 The Bahá'í Funeral Rite..129

    Chapter 9 Review 134

Chapter 10 Funerals and the U.S. Military Branches...135

    United States Flag Protocol – Proper Use of the Flag...143

    Fraternal Organizations for the Military 148

    Glossary for the Military Funeral Rite...151

    Chapter 10 Review..152

Chapter 11 Fraternal Organizations and the Funeral Rite 153

    The Masonic Funeral Rite 156

Basic Objectives of Funeral Service Personnel
~Locations~

1. Attention to Detail...10
2. Reverence for Sacred Objects..17
3. Appropriate Deference to Clergy/Officiants...30
4. Dignity and Decorum...49
5. Smoothness of Procedure..96
6. Flexibility and Adaptation to Culture and Customs..125
7. Awareness of Honorarium, Policy, and Fees..147
8. Awareness of Local, Regional, and Cultural Variations.....................................158

Chapter 1
The Protestant Funeral Rite – Liturgical

THE PROTESTANT FUNERAL RITE - LITURGICAL

Introduction to Protestantism

Unlike other religions and their accompanying funeral rites discussed in this text, the term *Protestant* is used to describe many different denominations. The Protestant classification will cover those churches which broke away from the Roman Catholic Church during the Reformation, or subsequent separations from these churches. While there are similarities among the various Protestant denominations, there are more areas in which they differ. This is true not just between denominations, but within denominations as well.

Before the funeral rite of a Protestant church can be described, the very term *Protestant* must be defined. For the purposes of our study, the term *Protestant* as it relates to membership defines any Western Christian who is not an adherent of the Roman Catholic Faith. Some of the denominations which are most often referred to in describing the Protestant tradition are: Baptist, Methodist, Church of Christ, Episcopal, Lutheran, Presbyterian, Assembly of God, Church of God, and Nazarene. Protestant traditions are first broken down by worship styles, and then classified as either Liturgical or Non-Liturgical.

Liturgical Protestant Churches

The funeral professional should be aware of four distinguishing characteristics of Liturgical Protestant denominations.

The first trait of the Liturgical Protestant denominations concerns the structure, or worship format, which they use. A Liturgical Protestant Church will have a prescribed order or form of worship which will be more or less consistent throughout the country or the world, all centered around the main event of worship – the Eucharist. (This is why these churches are sometimes also referred to as "Eucharist-centered" churches.) The order of worship will be

---

Helpful Terms

Denomination: a religious organization whose congregations are united in their adherence to its beliefs and practices

Protestant: any Western Christian who is not an adherent of the Roman Catholic Faith

Liturgical: "Eucharist-centered" denomination which has a prescribed order of worship or form of worship

Rubric: stated directions regarding church practices and procedures as approved by the church published in a special liturgical manual, hymnal, or book of prayer. The order of worship will also have the rubrics, or directions to be followed, for that service listed immediately prior to the service. As a result, a member of one Liturgical Protestant Church – Lutheran, for example – can attend another church of the same denomination and easily follow the service because of their liturgical style of worship. This is not to say that minor variations due to parochial or pastoral desires do not occur. However, these variations are usually inconsequential and cause the worshiper little inconvenience. Another classic example of a Liturgical Protestant Church is the Episcopal Church.

> **What is the difference in "church" and "Church"?**
>
> For our purposes, "church" with a lower case *c* refers either to a facility of worship or a local congregation. The capitalized word "Church," on the other hand," will refer to the adherents of a particular faith as a whole group.

The second trait of Liturgical Protestant Churches is based on the layout of the worship facility. One that is designed and built *liturgically* is one which is built in the shape of a cross. The cross bars form the transepts, or wings, at the front of the church (see diagram below). The

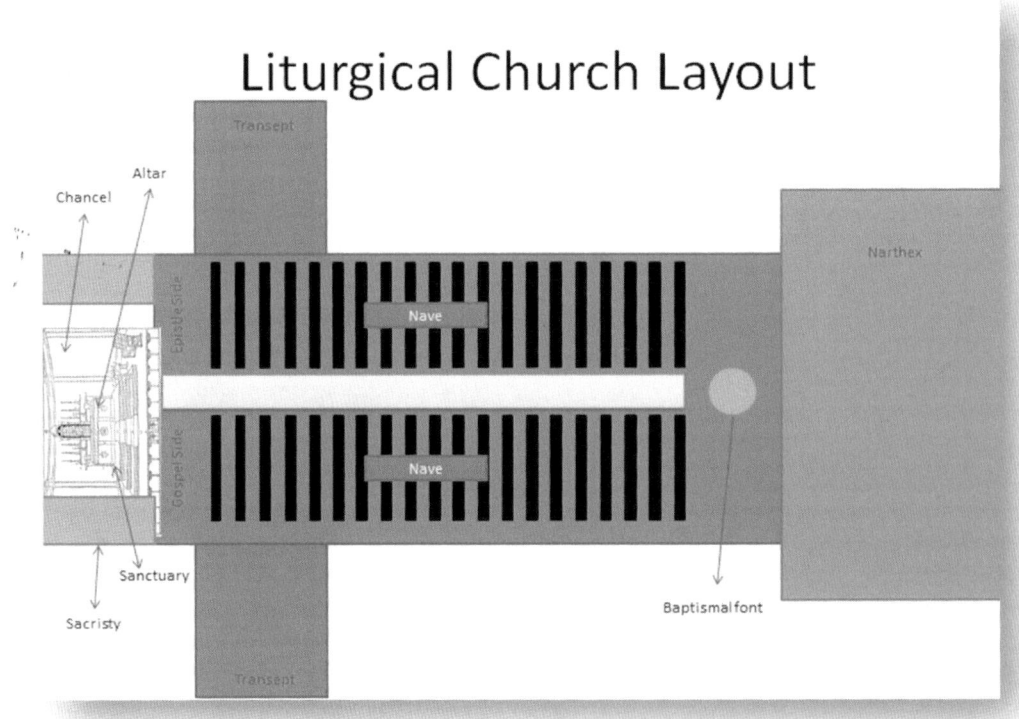

Chapter 1: The Protestant Funeral Rite – Liturgical page 3

> **Helpful Terms**
>
> *Gospel side*: the left side of the church (as the congregation faces the altar) from which the minister delivers the sermon
>
> *Epistle side*: the right side of the church (as the congregation faces the altar) from which readings and prayers are often proclaimed

focal point of a Liturgical Protestant Church is the cross or crucifix, either centered on the altar or immediately above the altar. It will also have a center aisle with direct approach to the altar through the communion rail. In some instances, the communion rail may be closed but allow access around either end. It should be noted that today many churches which are liturgical in their style of worship have constructed their worship facilities with more creative architectural styles while still maintaining the center aisle and crucifix as the focal point.

Thirdly, there is a direct connection in Liturgical Protestant Churches between the liturgical style of worship and architecture. These churches will have certain locations designed for readings, prayers, or recitations. Rather than a single lectern centered in the front of the church from which the minister will speak, the Liturgical Church architecture provides for two lecterns. Although there will be some variations in the placement of these lecterns, the lectern located on the left side (as the congregation faces the altar) is typically designated as the *Gospel Lectern*, while the lectern located on the right side is designated as the *Epistle Lectern*. Traditionally, the minister delivers sermons from the Gospel side, and readings and prayers are performed on the Epistle side.

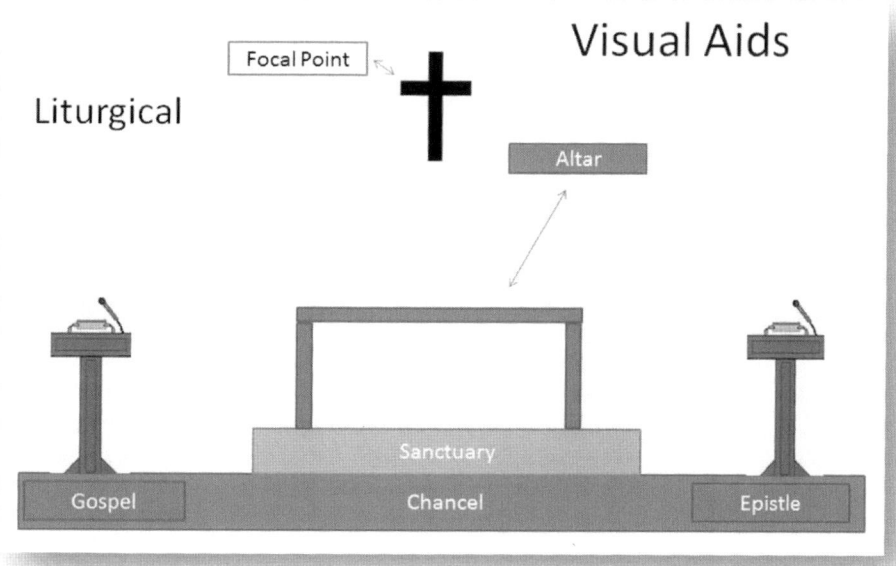

Finally, the Liturgical Protestant Church utilizes religious paraphernalia during its regular worship services and funeral rites. These visual symbols are maintained by the altar attendants, or *acolytes*. The more religious implements that are utilized, the more people will necessarily be part of the funeral processional and recessional. The function and placement of the acolytes will be discussed in the specific chapters dealing with Liturgical Churches.

Notification of the Clergy

Those churches which are classified as Liturgical Protestant will have varied local, cultural, and personal preferences as to ministerial notification. On the whole, there is usually no requirement for the funeral professional to contact the local minister; however, individual circumstances may determine the funeral professional's role. Depending on the size of the community being served, the funeral professional may work with any number of Liturgical Protestant communities. It becomes necessary for the funeral professional to establish a line of communication with the various ministers within these communities in order to determine their preferences on such matters as the notification of the death of a congregation member. The funeral professional should realize the importance of establishing and maintaining good inter-professional relationships with the clergy of all religious communities.

Removal of the Remains

There are no restrictions based on church doctrine as to the removal of the remains of members of Liturgical Protestant Churches. There may be restrictions for the removal from the

place of death due to the cause or manner of the death, or in order to meet some other civil requirements, but not due to or affecting the religious beliefs or membership of the deceased.

> **Protestantism: Bruised, Broken, or Completely Fractured?**
>
> From the outside, the variety of Protestant denominations may seem to indicate a severe dysfunction within Christianity. The heart of the Protestant movement is still "Reformation." This spirit of reformation affects denominations' religious, social, and cultural views and activities as society progresses. These groups still have similar, or in some cases the same, orthodox views of Christianity, yet focus on unique traits which set them apart from other groups. These traits are part of their continual "reforming" or purification principles which remain constant within the denomination. Reformers keep traditions which they think have become "lost"; i.e. churches which still practice immersion as the preferred method of baptism. Reformers also add principles which have become "lost," i.e. the Holiness movement's view of the work of the Holy Spirit in gifts and healing. Some denominations focus on the eternal state of man (evangelical), while others focus on the present state of man (social gospel). Is Protestantism completely fractured, somewhat broken, or just bruised? The answer is – none of the above. It is a dynamic, living movement which has the ability to adapt to cultural, societal, and religious changes.
>
> **SO WHAT?** Many families today have few links with religious organizations. It is not unusual for a family to want a "religious" service, without considering all that entails. The funeral professional is usually the first to determine what type of service would comfort an at-need family. For some, the evangelistic funeral service may be the key to bringing closure. For others, a message from a social perspective may be what is needed. When the family asks you to help to provide the appropriate minister, will you be able to meet their need?

Preparation of the Remains

No Liturgical Protestant Church places mandates on the method or extent to which the deceased's remains should be prepared prior to disposition. In most instances, as with other religions, the fact that the decedent belonged to a particular church would increase the likelihood that a funeral service with a viewing would take place. This would dictate that some preparation of the body would be needed in order to allow time for the planning of the actual service.

Dressing and Casketing the Remains

The choice of clothing to be worn by the deceased and the type of casket to be used are left up to the family. There are no written doctrinal preferences among Liturgical Protestant

Churches regarding funeral dress or casket regulations. Usually, the family will provide clothing they deem most appropriate.

Pre-service Considerations

The deceased's denominational background will play a role in determining the location of the visitation and funeral. For those choosing to utilize the funeral home chapel, the seating and positioning of the casket will be similar to all Protestant funeral traditions. The preferences of the officiating minister will usually determine the use and amount of flowers displayed in the chapel, as well as whether to have an "open" or "closed" casket.

If the funeral service is going to be at the church, the funeral professional should have working knowledge of the layout and amenities of the facility. The funeral professional should have a level of competence when working in a religious venue even if the church provides ushers and attendants to assist the funeral guests. The funeral professional should also have specific permission and direction on how to make the facility comfortable for the families they serve. This knowledge will assist in determining optimal placement of flower arrangements, as well as where to seat the family, casket bearers, honorary casket bearers, and fraternal organizations. It will also aid in determining the processional, casket placement, and the recessional.

> **Advance Scouting**
>
> New facilities, remodeled facilities, or ministerial changes:
>
> One of the lost arts of funeral directing is the advance scout. Sadly, this vital practice which was once considered so important as to be done days in advance, has more recently been shifted to a quick survey just before the service.
>
> The scout should get permission to walk through the facility prior to the church preparations for the visitation or funeral. He or she should ask pertinent questions regarding traditional seating areas, casket preferences, and logistics for flower and casket delivery. Once this information is obtained, it can be used to pre-plan the equipment and staffing needs for the service.
>
> This type of pre-planning prevents the last-minute scramble to gather equipment and personnel. It also goes a long way in developing credibility with families and religious communities.

Often it will be necessary to move certain items of furniture when a funeral is to be held in the church. Funeral home staff should always seek permission prior to moving any furnishings and be certain to replace them after the service. It is also good public relations to attempt to pick up flower petals, tissues, service folders, and other items which may have been left behind following the service rather than leaving it for the church cleaning crew.

The Funeral Service

If the funeral service is to be held in the church, it is more likely that the service will follow a Liturgical order of worship. The use of candles and incense are common practice in some Liturgical Protestant Churches. The rubrics or procedures which the service will follow may be found in the hymnal, a separate handbook, or a prayer book. Normally these will already be distributed for use during the service. It is a good idea, however, for the funeral professional to check with the clergy beforehand to be certain.

Many Liturgical Protestant Churches use a *pall* to cover the casket during the funeral service. The pall is normally draped over the casket just prior to the processional when the casket is moved into the nave from the narthex. The leader of the processional will be the *crucifer*, who leads the procession down the aisle carrying a cross or crucifix. The *officiant* will generally follow the crucifer, followed by a member of the funeral home staff, the casket, and casket bearers. Depending on the width of the aisle, the casket bearers will either walk in front of the casket or alongside the casket. Another funeral home staff member and the family will follow the casket. While the crucifer and clergy move to their respective positions at or around the altar, the funeral professional will position the casket and seat the casket bearers and the family.

> **Helpful Terms**
>
> *Pall*: a symbolic cloth covering placed over the casket as it moves from the nave to the narthex signifying the righteousness of Christ bestowed at baptism and equality in the eyes of God
>
> *Crucifer*: one who carries the crucifix in a religious procession
>
> *Officiant*: one who conducts a religious service or ceremony

The order of worship for a Liturgical Protestant service will vary depending on the denomination and the preferences of the officiant. An example of some of the activities which might be included in a Liturgical Protestant funeral are Scripture reading and

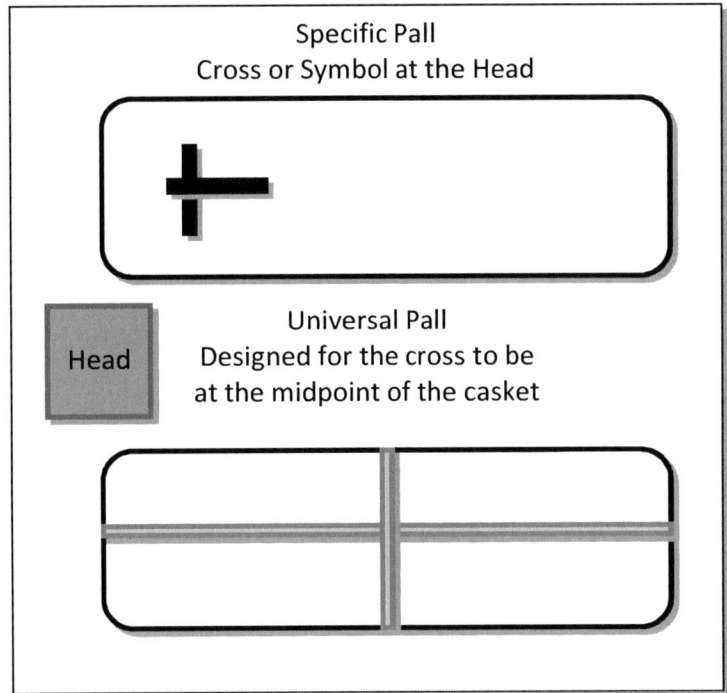

prayer, a musical selection, a eulogy and/or obituary, a sermon, another musical selection, a prayer, and a benediction. Some of these activities will take place at the altar; others from the Gospel and Epistle Lecterns.

Following the benediction, the crucifer, officiant, casket, casket bearers, and family typically move in a recessional back out of the church. The recessional order is the same as the processional into the church. If a pall is being used, it will be removed in the narthex of the church, and a casketpiece or flag will be placed back on the casket before it is moved out to the waiting automobiles.

In most cases the officiant at a Liturgical Protestant Church will wear vestments during services, including funeral services. Following the funeral service, the officiant may change out of the vestments prior to going to the cemetery or place of the committal service. If acolytes are used as part of the service, one or more may also be expected to go to the site of the committal service. The funeral professional will need to ascertain these facts in advance in order to allow space for them in the funeral cortege, if necessary.

The Committal Service

The method of final disposition may be *interment* (earth burial), *entombment* (placement in a mausoleum), cremation, burial at sea, or donation of the body to science. The type of disposition will largely determine the role of both the officiant and the funeral professional in the committal service. For example, if final disposition is to result in cremation, the committal service may take place at the site of the funeral service at the conclusion of the funeral rather than moving to the cemetery.

With the majority of dispositions still being interments, the usual procedure is to proceed to the cemetery and, once at the cemetery, move in a procession led by the officiant to the grave. After the casket is placed on the lowering device, the casket bearers positioned, and the family seated, the officiant will conduct a short graveside service. This service usually consists of Scripture reading, prayer, and the making of the sign of the cross on the casket with sand or flower petals, concluding with a benediction.

Basic Objectives of Funeral Service Professionals
Objective 1

"Attention to Detail"

Deceased and Casket:

Does the deceased's make-up need refreshing (whether the casket will be opened or not)? Is the casket straight on the church trucks? Has the casket been wiped down to remove fingerprints, smears, or flowers?

Flower Placement:

Are the family pieces in the correct location? Has flower placement blocked the view of the officiant or others?

Environmental Awareness:

Is the air or heat at the appropriate level for the number in attendance? Should you have people in the parking lot to aid elderly or handicapped family or guests? Is the cemetery area clear of hazards (holes, wet markers, etc.)?

Courtesy Reminders:

Have the participants been verified? Are you prepared for an absent or late participant?

Church Case:

Do you have enough "reserved" signs? Do you need multiple guest books for multiple entrances into the facility? Are the boutonnieres fresh?

Think about this: Planning a service is simple compared to proper execution of the family's wishes. Families will often forget the big things (who sang, ministerial message, time frame). They will remember, however, those small details and the preventable mistakes or omissions.

The Episcopal Funeral Rite

Introduction to the Episcopal Church

The Episcopal Church is one of the traditionally Liturgical denominations. With its roots in the Catholic tradition around 314 C.E., the Anglicans (so called because of their descendancy from the Church of England) were separated from the Catholic Pope by declaration of King Henry VIII (1534 C.E.).

> **Helpful Terms**
>
> *Anglican*: term originating circa 1246 from the Latin term *ecclesia anglicana* (English Church)
>
> The date of 314 is an approximate date when Christianity was accepted. (St. Alban was the first Christian martyr in 304 C.E.).

Although part of the worldwide Anglican Communion, only the churches in the United States and Scotland use the word Episcopal, which comes from the Greek word *episkopos,* meaning "bishops." This emphasizes the role of the bishop as the chief symbol of the continuity with the Church of all ages and as the chief pastor.

The Episcopal Church has both Catholic and Protestant ties. They retain all of the ancient sacraments, creeds, and orders of the Catholic Church while rejecting the idea that the Bishop of Rome (the Pope) has authority over the Church.

The Episcopal Church was formed in the United States in 1789, and there are approximately two million U.S. Episcopalians today. ("Baptized Members by Province and Dioceses 2000-2010," The Episcopal Church, October 31, 2011, p.3, retrieved April 26, 2014.)

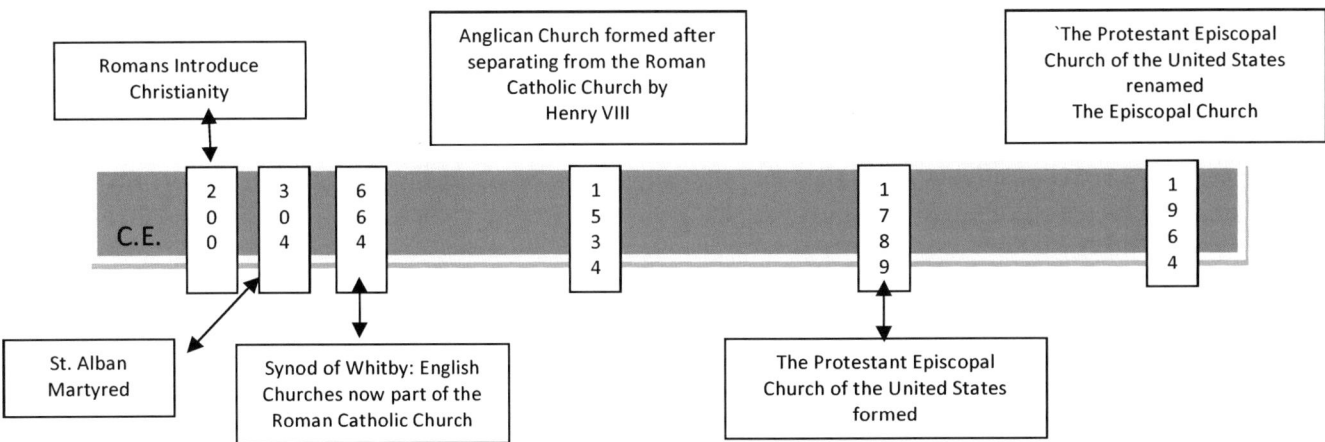

Notification of Death

Although it is not necessary to notify the clergy prior to or at the time of death, it is a generally accepted practice, and priests usually appreciate timely notification. The Episcopal Church practices *extreme unction*, or anointing of the sick, along with communion for those who are dying. The local congregation will likely be aware of those individuals who die due to a lingering illness.

> **Helpful Term**
>
> *Extreme Unction- Anointing of the sick:* the use of oil, holy water, or hands to bless those who are in danger of losing life

Removal of the Remains

There are no restrictions for the removal of the remains of lay members of the Episcopal Church. However, there may be restrictions for certain members of the clergy (bishops, priests, or deacons) or for different orders.

> **To notify or not to notify, that is the question.**
>
> The funeral professional is not obligated to make the call to the parish at the time of death. It should be noted that there is a tradition within the Episcopal community regarding clergy contact with the funeral director prior to family involvement.
>
> Data published by The Episcopal Diocese of New York encourages the families to contact their parish priest prior to making contact with the funeral professional. This initial contact will allow the priest to counsel the family in religious requirements of the "discipline and worship" of the local parish. It also suggests that the priest should make initial contact on behalf of the family (ideally).
>
> Source: The Episcopal Diocese of New York, "Concerning Funerals: Funeral Practices in the Episcopal Church for use by: Clergy, Laity and Morticians," www.dioceseny.org/pages/231-concerningfunerals: Retrieved April 28, 2014.

Preparation of the Remains

There are no guidelines as to the type or amount of preparations which are to take place. Since members of the Episcopal Church accept interment, entombment, and cremation as viable means of final disposition, the use of embalming may or may not be desired. The preference of the family will determine the extent of the preparation of the remains.

Dressing and Casketing

There are no restrictions as to the type of clothing or casket to be used for lay persons. Members of the clergy or certain orders of the

Episcopal Church may prefer the use of their ritual vestments. The type of casket to be used for a member of the clergy is generally left up to the family.

Pre-service Considerations

For those families choosing a traditional funeral, it is customary to hold visitation at the funeral home. No special equipment is needed for the visitation. Flowers may be displayed during the visitation at the funeral home.

The Funeral Service

It is strongly encouraged that the funeral service be held in the Episcopal Church. With the exception of altar flowers, flowers are generally not displayed when the funeral is held in the church. The funeral service begins with the processional of the pall-covered casket into the

church. The casket is led into the church by the crucifer, followed by the bishop or priest, the casket bearers with the casket, and the family.

The Episcopal Church is classified as a Liturgical Protestant Church, and as such will follow a prescribed order of worship which will be more or less consistent everywhere. In the Episcopal Church the order of worship will be found in *The Book of Common Prayer*.

Prior to the funeral service, or as a part of the service, the celebration of the Holy Eucharist (Holy Communion) may be observed. This celebration provides the observers with an opportunity to thank God for all of His blessings as well as to pray for the soul of the deceased.

The focus on the sermon at an Episcopal funeral is to teach the Church's beliefs concerning death. The basis of this belief centers on the view that death is the beginning of a new life, reunited with God. No eulogy as such is usually given as it is considered the "prerogative of God to judge and commend."

The use of hymns is commonly practiced with the congregation singing songs dealing with the Resurrection and God the Son's victory over sin and death.

At the conclusion of the funeral service the casket is taken from the church in the recessional and the pall is removed prior to being placed in the funeral coach. The placement of flowers or the American flag on the casket may occur at this point, if so desired by the family.

Since cremation is an accepted means of disposition, this may affect the type of funeral service held. If a traditional service is to be held prior to the cremation, the funeral service described above will generally remain unchanged, with the exception that the committal service may take place in the church at the end of the funeral service, and there may not be a recessional. In some areas, if cremation is to be the final means of disposition, the use of a memorial service instead of the traditional funeral service may occur.

> **Is the Episcopal Church catholic?**
>
> The answer is ... yes *and* no.
>
> The term *catholic* means "universal." All baptized members of the Episcopal community are part of the Episcopal Church (universal). This means that adherents can partake of sacraments in any Episcopal fellowship (local). However, they are not part of the Roman Catholic Church, which has distinctive traits separate from the Episcopal community.
>
> Therefore, it can be said that the Episcopal Church is both Protestant and catholic.

The Committal Service

If interment or entombment is chosen as the final means of disposition, the committal service will likely be held at the cemetery or mausoleum. The committal service will typically consist of a prayer, a short Scripture reading, and the symbolic committal of the casketed remains to its final resting place. The priest will often use sand or flower petals to make the sign of the cross on the closed casket.

Because that's the way we've *always* done it!

Why do you encourage "religious" families to have a wake, vigil, or visitation prior to the service? If your answer is "because it is traditional," you have missed the theological principles guiding your Christian families.

The service (liturgy) is a God-centered activity, an opportunity for the grieving community to come together to worship (corporate responsive praise) the glorious achievements of Christ, and the certain hope of a resurrection. However, the wake, vigil, or visitation is individual-centered. It is a time of devotion. Churches want their members to be with the deceased and personally focus upon the meaning of life, death, and faith. It is a time of personal, private communion with their Savior.

The combination of personal and corporate worship that these two services provide is vital to the Christian faith. Death cannot hinder either community or personal faith, and you help facilitate the expression of that faith in this way.

The Episcopal Church	
Classification	Liturgical Protestant
Origin	Henry VIII
Clergy Notification	not required; extreme unction practiced
Removal	no restrictions
Preparation of Remains	no restriction (interment/entombment/cremation)
Dressing and Casketing	no restrictions: clergy may wear vestments
Pre-Service	no restrictions; no religious paraphernalia; flowers permitted
Funeral Service	
Place of Service	church encouraged
Processional	crucifer, bishop or priest, casket bearers with palled casket, and family
Rubric	*The Book of Common Prayer*
Communion	prior to, or as part of, the funeral
Eulogy	none
Flowers	limited
Music	congregational
Recessional	same as processional
Committal Service	committal service at place of disposition; prayer; Scripture reading; minister places sand or flower petals in the sign of the cross

The Lutheran Funeral Rite

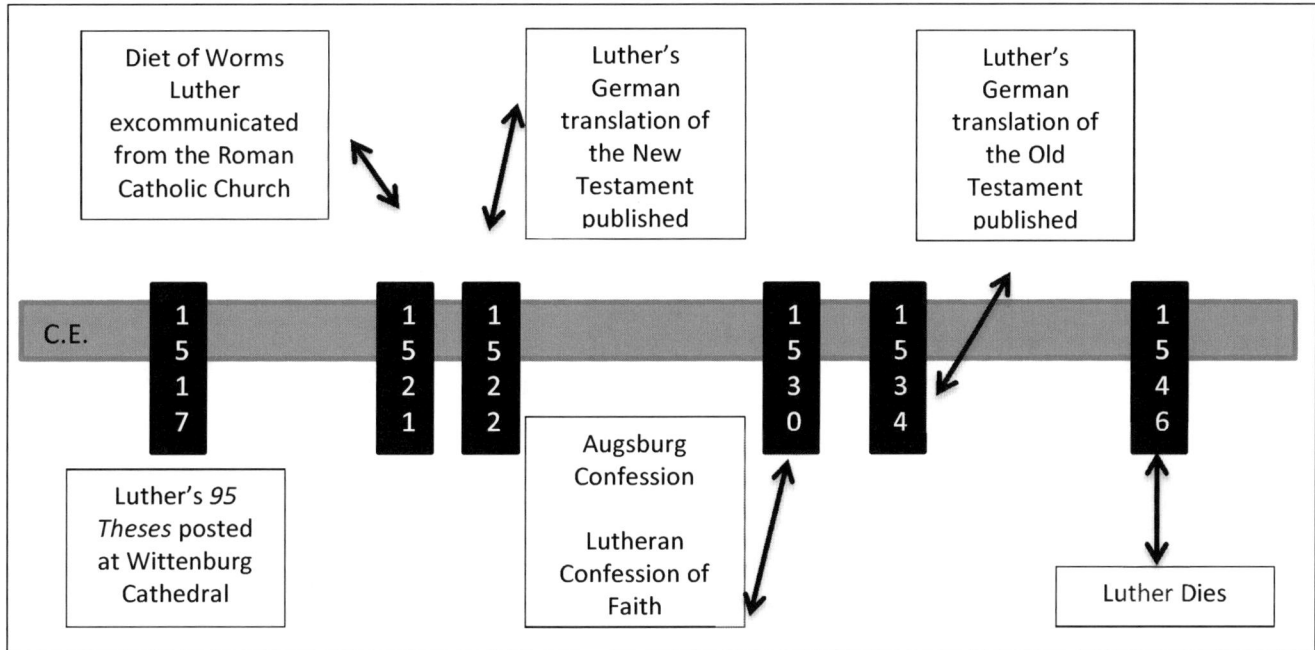

Introduction to the Lutheran Church

The Lutheran Church began in 1517 as a protest by one man, Martin Luther, a Roman Catholic priest, who refused to abide by certain demands of the Pope of the Catholic Church. The actions taken by Martin Luther marked the beginning, not only of the Lutheran Church, but also of the Protestant movement.

> **Helpful Terms**
>
> *Synod*: ecclesiastic assembly, made up of bishops or delegates to assist in Church government
>
> *Ecclesiastic*: of or related to the church or clergy
>
> *Autocephalous*: self-governing

Today there are nine million Lutherans belonging to different *synods,* or branches, of the Lutheran Church. Although each synod elects their leader through a democratic process, these leaders serve limited terms under constitutional authority. Within each synod, the local congregation owns their own property and building, and is self-governing (*autocephalous*) in its local affairs.

In recent years there have been a number of mergers of synods in the United States. Today the largest body of Lutherans belongs to the Evangelical Lutheran Church in America with approximately 5.9 million members. The Missouri Synod has approximately 3 million members. These two synods then account for approximately 90% of the Lutherans in North America.

The primary differences between the various synods are mainly those of observable rites and ceremonies. The doctrines or basic beliefs upon which the churches are founded remain similar. However, the funeral professional will find that funeral rites may vary even among the Lutheran Churches within his or her community, especially when more than one synod is present.

Basic Objectives of Funeral Service Professionals
Objective 2

"Reverence for Sacred Objects"

Would you kiss an icon at an Eastern Orthodox Church? Would you bow or genuflect before the tabernacle when entering a Roman Catholic Church? Would you treat the Star of David and Menorah with the same respect you would a cross or crucifix? Would you treat the Imam's Koran with the same respect you would a Holy Bible? Would you treat the Buddhist altar differently than you would a Liturgical altar?

The answer to these questions will say a lot about your willingness to serve the various religious groups in your community.

Funeral professionals practice an *ethic of hospitality*. This is a religious ethic found in all major religious groups. It permits individuals from different traditions and backgrounds (*strangers* in the Old Testament) to come together for a common purpose without being asked to sacrifice anything. Kissing the icon does not detract from one's personal beliefs. Treating other religious symbols with respect does not diminish one's view of their own symbols. Funeral directing is an others-centered service.

Think about this: Showing this kindness to various communities of faith actually strengthens their respect for you and your funeral firm. So what kind of person do you want the community to see, both as a funeral professional and a community leader?

Notification of Death

Unless otherwise expressed by a local pastor, it is usually not necessary to notify the pastor at the time a death occurs. The family's relationship with the church and/or the pastor will often determine the point at which the pastor is notified. In some cases, the family may wish him to be present at the time of death, while in other situations he may not be notified until arrangements are being made.

Removal of Remains

There are no restrictions or requirements imposed by church officials when a member of the Lutheran Church dies. The funeral home staff can expect to make the removal from the place of death when notified by the local civil authorities that the body is ready to be released.

Preparation of Remains

The preparation of the remains is usually based on the choices made by the family. Embalming is permitted and often chosen by the family.

Dressing and Casketing the Remains

The choices of clothing to be worn by the deceased and the type of casket to be used are left entirely up to the family. The Lutheran Church does not place any special requirements as to the clothing or the type of casket.

Pre-Service Considerations

Traditionally, the funeral was held in the church, and this is still a preference among many Lutheran pastors and families. This is not, however, a Church requirement and the location of the funeral service is left up to the family. Since Lutheran churches are liturgical in their worship style, the location of the funeral will play a role in the type of funeral service held. Flowers may be permitted in the church.

The Funeral Service

If the funeral is held in the church, much of the religious paraphernalia that accompany Liturgical services will be used. With the altar as the focal point in the church, the use of acolytes, a cross, candles, a pall, and, in some congregations, incense, are part of the funeral service. Rubrics will be found in the hymnal and other special readings will be followed.

The use of the pall dictates a closed casket during the funeral service, which often results in viewing the deceased in the narthex of the church prior to the beginning of the funeral service. The crucifer will lead the procession into the church, followed by the pastor, the casket bearers with the casket, and the family. The funeral professionals should be interspersed in the procession to assist in seating the casket bearers and family. The funeral professionals will also see to the positioning of the casket, either parallel or at right

---

Lutheran View of Cremation

In the previous edition of this publication, cremation was listed as being discouraged among the practitioners of the Lutheran community.

According to Chris Duckworth, writing for the Evangelical Lutheran Church in America (ECLA), "cremation is a perfectly appropriate way to care for the remains of the deceased." Dignified disposition of the remains are still encouraged, whether burial at sea or earth burial.

"A Pastor's Approach to Funerals" (article)
Living Lutheran: Lively Engagement in Faith & Life
www.elca.org/en/Living-Lutheran/Seeds/2013/03/130313
Retrieved 04/27/14

The Lutheran Church Missouri Synod (LCMS) has added instructions for the committal of a person's ashes to *The Lutheran Service Book*.

It should be noted that this acceptance is not without its detractors. Some ministers still oppose cremation on theological grounds. It would be best for the funeral director to check with the minister(s) of local congregations (see article below).

Blogs.lcms.org/2008/cremation-not-a-christian-option-8-2008

angles to the altar. Communion may be offered as part of the funeral service if it is the wish of the family. At the conclusion of the funeral, the recessional will return the funeral party to their automobiles for the trip to the site of the committal service. While the use of cremation is still not accepted by all congregations within the Lutheran Church, it is permitted by the Evangelical Church in America (ECLA).

If the funeral is held in the funeral home or a location other than a Lutheran church, the funeral service will more closely resemble a Non-Liturgical Protestant service. The use of rubrics, acolytes, the pall, incense, the processional, and recessional may be eliminated outside of the church facility.

The Committal Service

Recently, the use of cremation has been more accepted among the Lutheran synods. However, interment or entombment is most often the preferred means of final disposition for members of the Lutheran Church. The committal service will usually include prayer, Scripture reading, and the committal of the body to its final resting place. Flower petals or earth may be used to make the sign of the cross upon the casket.

A wide variety of customs and other factors can influence Lutheran funerals. These factors may include anything from the nationality of the congregation to the particular synod the deceased was a member of, or even local customs. The funeral professional should arrange a meeting with the various pastors of the Lutheran congregations to be served in order to determine customs and traditions of the local congregations and individual preferences of the pastors involved.

The Lutheran Church	
Classification	Liturgical Protestant
Origin	Martin Luther
Clergy Notification	not required
Removal	no restrictions
Preparation of Remains	no restrictions
	interment, entombment, cremation
Dressing and Casketing	no restrictions
	clergy may wear vestments
Pre-Service	no restrictions
	no religious paraphernalia
	flowers permitted
Funeral Service	
Place of Service	church encouraged for communion
Processional	crucifer, bishop or priest, casket bearers with palled casket, and family
Rubric	*Lutheran Book of Worship,*
	Hymnal of Lutheran Worship,
	Lutheran Service Book
Communion	prior to, or as part of the funeral
Eulogy	permitted
Flowers	permitted
Music	congregational
Recessional	same as processional
Committal Service	committal service at place of disposition
	prayer, Scripture reading
	minister places sand or flower pedals in the sign of the cross

Glossary of Liturgical Protestant Terms

ACOLYTE: an altar attendant (may be male or female)

ALTAR: an elevated place or structure on which sacrifices are offered or at which religious rites are performed; the table from which Holy Communion is served and prayers are offered

BENEDICTION: a ritual blessing offered at the conclusion of a service

BOOK OF COMMON PRAYER: the text containing recitations, prayers, and prescribed orders of worship in the Episcopal Church

CHANCEL: the area around the altar of the church, usually enclosing the clergy and other officials

CRUCIFER: one who carries the processional cross in an ecclesiastical procession

ECCLESIASTICAL: referring to the church or clergy

ECUMENICAL: an epithet applied to a council regarded as representing the whole of Christendom

EPISTLE SIDE: the right side of the church (as the congregation faces the altar), from which readings and prayers are often proclaimed

EUCHARIST-CENTERED WORSHIP: see also *Liturgical Worship*; the prescribed order or form of worship used by some churches in which the Eucharist or Holy Communion is the central element

EXTREME UNCTION: in the Episcopal faith, the use of oil, holy water, or hands to bless those who are in danger of losing life

GOSPEL SIDE: the left side of the church (as the congregation faces the altar), from which sermons are preached

LITURGICAL WORSHIP: see also *Eucharist-Centered Worship*; the prescribed order or form of worship used by some churches in which the Eucharist or Holy Communion is the central element

NARTHEX: see also *Vestibule*; the entryway to the church proper

NAVE: the main body of the church where seating is provided

NON-LITURGICAL WORSHIP: see also *Scripture-Centered Worship*; a form or order of worship having the scriptures as the central element, with the actual order of worship determined by the local congregation or clergy

PALL: a symbolic cloth covering placed on the casket representing both the righteousness of Christ bestowed at one's baptism and the equality of all men before God

Parochial: belonging to a parish; restricted to a parish; limited in range or scope

Protestant: any Western Christian who is not an adherent to the Roman Catholic Church

Rubrics: printed or stated directions regarding church practices and procedures as approved by religious leadership

Sanctuary: liturgically, the part of the church containing the altar (or, if there are several altars, the high altar); commonly, a holy or sacred place devoted to the worship of any deity; historically, a place of refuge

Scripture-Centered Worship: see also *Non-Liturgical Worship*; a form or order of worship having the scriptures as the central element, with the actual order of worship determined by the local congregation or clergy

Transepts: the wings of the main part of the church, which may serve as small chapels for baptisms, weddings, and even small funeral services

Vestibule: see also *Narthex*; the entryway to the church proper

Vestments: ritual garments of the clergy

Chapter 1 Review

1. What are the four characteristics of Liturgical Protestant denominations?
2. Moving from the narthex to the altar, describe the architectural layout of a Liturgical Protestant church.
3. Use the following terms to describe the chancel: gospel side, epistle side, altar, sanctuary, and focal point.
4. List the participants in a Liturgical procession, in order.
5. What is the purpose of a pall?
6. Who is considered the founder of the Anglican church?
7. What is the Episcopal Church's stance on eulogies?
8. What is the rubric of the Episcopal Church?
9. Who is the founder of the Lutheran Church?
10. What is the Lutheran Church's stance on cremation?
11. Review special requirements for notification of clergy, removal of remains, preparation of remains, and dressing and casketing for each group included in this chapter.
12. Define the following terms:
    a. Protestant
    b. Eucharist-centered
    c. Scripture-centered
    d. Rubric
    e. Gospel side
    f. Epistle side
    g. Acolyte
    h. Pall
    i. Crucifer
    j. Extreme unction
    k. Synod

Chapter 2
The Protestant Funeral Rite – Non-Liturgical

The Protestant Funeral Rite – Non-Liturgical

Introduction to Non-Liturgical Protestantism

A Non-Liturgical Protestant Church is defined as one that is simple in its worship style. Non-Liturgical facilities are built in a variety of styles ranging from traditional to modern. The fact that no religious paraphernalia are utilized in their worship means that these congregations can practice their rites at almost any location.

Most Protestant churches are classified as Non-Liturgical both in their architecture and in their style of worship. The Non-Liturgical Protestant church is one which, as a church body, has no set or prescribed order of service or worship, but leaves the actual form or order to the discretion of the pastor in charge. These churches may have suggested orders of worship for some of the more formal services, but these are suggestions only. They will in many instances conform quite closely to set patterns of worship, but inasmuch as they are not church approved and required of all churches within that particular denomination, they are not considered as liturgical by definition. For example, you may find a similarity among Baptist services, but the fact that they do not have to follow a set order of worship makes them Non-Liturgical. Other examples of Non-Liturgical Protestant churches include Methodist, Church of Christ, Assembly of God, Church of God, and Nazarene.

> **How do I address the minister?**
>
> Great question!
>
> *Reverend* is usually the most acceptable term for Non-Liturgical ministers. This title is used in print more than in oral practice (as in, "The Reverend Mr., Mrs., or Miss").
>
> *Bishop* is also utilized in organizations which have a hierarchical system within the church or within the denomination.
>
> *Pastor* is very common if the minister is the leader of a congregation.
>
> *Brother* and *Sister* are also common usage among Non-Liturgical Protestants.
>
> **Still confused?** It is simple really – just ask how they would prefer to be addressed. Remember there will be both printable titles and oral preferences.

Notification of the Clergy

With the decision making process of Non-Liturgical Protestant churches resting primarily with the clergy, the funeral professional should determine the preferences of each individual minister in order to maintain a smooth working relationship. If notification is required, it is usually on a case-by-case basis.

Removal of Remains

Protestants do not place any restrictions on the removal of remains from the place of death. The cause or manner of the death may affect removal, but religious factors will not.

Preparation of Remains

Embalming is accepted and allowed by most Non-Liturgical Protestant organizations. The choice of whether or not the body is to be embalmed is left entirely up to the family. For most Protestants the concept of Christian freedom is the main directive. It permits families to make decisions which are neither biblically commanded nor forbidden.

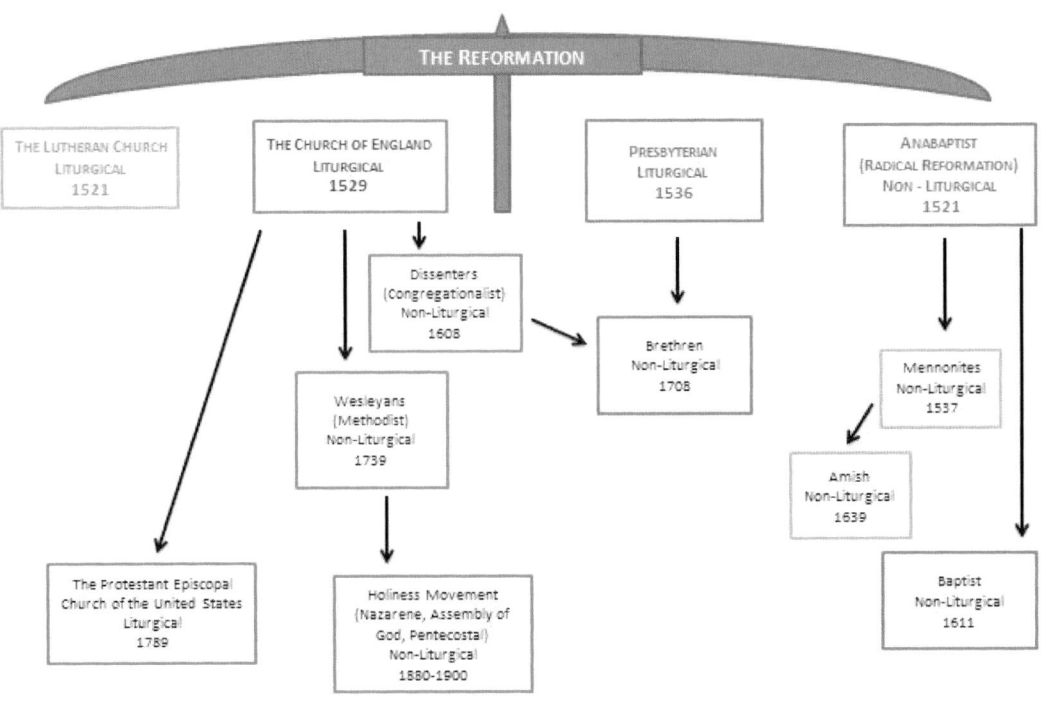

Dressing and Casketing the Remains

There are no special requirements or restrictions as to the type of clothing for Non-Liturgical Protestant churches. The deceased's clothing or clothing purchased at the funeral home are the usual choices made by the family. Likewise, there are no special requirements or restrictions as to the type of casket used. The choice is left up to the family, and is based on their personal preferences.

Pre-Service Considerations

The clergy of Non-Liturgical Protestant denominations usually determine the order of worship based on their own preferences. For this reason, many variations in services are possible. This makes it even more important for the funeral professional to meet with each member of the clergy in advance, if possible, to determine their preferences. Building these relationships ahead of time will assist the funeral professional when planning funeral services with or for members of that particular congregation.

There will likely be minimal differences between a funeral held in the funeral home and one held in a Non-Liturgical Protestant church. The fact that these churches do not use rubrics, candles, religious paraphernalia, acolytes, or a pall creates more similarity between the services held in either location. Also, as in most funeral home

---

> **"Didn't they teach you that in seminary?"**
>
> Since Non-Liturgical Protestants do not utilize rubrics, funerals are most often covered as academic theory rather than practical application in a seminary setting. Many times this involves more administrative training rather than practical instruction. Practical application occurs during the minister's apprenticeship or as a student assistant.
>
> When a young minister (he or she) approaches you and asks you to develop the service, what will you do? Replying with "That's not my job" is not an option. Here is a standard service you may suggest.
>
> Opening Prayer
>
> Song
>
> Obituary / Eulogy
>
> Song
>
> Message
>
> Benediction
>
> This skeleton outline can easily be adapted for extra speakers or songs.
>
> **NOTE**: *Never* tell the family this is the minister's first funeral, and advise him/her not to say anything along those lines. The service is about the family, not the minister. They will be accepting to his/her generous message in their time of need.

chapels, the prayers, readings, eulogies, and sermon will be delivered from a single pulpit. In addition, most clergy will choose to wear their normal dress clothing rather than vestments. However, it should be noted that some Non-Liturgical clergy still prefer to wear a robe for formal services.

In spite of the similarities between services held at the funeral home and in a Non-Liturgical church, the wise funeral professional will still become familiar with the various Non-Liturgical Protestant churches he or she will serve. This will assist the funeral professional in discussing seating arrangements and logistical matters during the arrangement conference. As with all outside services, he/she should also gain knowledge of the amenities and permissions needed to adjust the environment for the family's comfort. The funeral professional should also determine the policy governing the use and/or placement of flowers in these facilities, parking availability, and so on.

The Funeral Service

The variances among the many Non-Liturgical denominations are due to the lack of formal procedures, architectural design, and personal preferences. The lack of formality also allows the funeral service to be at any location of the family's choosing. The services themselves will have similar

Ecumenical Services

Ecumenical services occasionally bring together several ministers from different Christian backgrounds. These services are designed to assist families of different Christian affiliations. With few exceptions, ministers from various denominations tend to work well in this environment.

Since the "hope" of Christianity is the resurrection and reunion with Christ, most denominations focus on this similar theme in funerals. If the decedent is Roman Catholic and the children are Protestant, they may have a Protestant vigil, with a Roman Catholic Mass. For Non-Liturgical Protestants, a Presbyterian minister may be welcomed to speak during the ceremony at the local Baptist church.

The funeral professional plays a vital role with families in planning these services. When contacting the clergy, they must be made aware of the family's wishes and their particular role in the service (obituary reading, prayer, homily, scripture reading, etc.). The funeral professional should also encourage dialogue among the participants to ensure a seamless service free of misunderstandings.

elements (prayers, eulogies, songs, sermon, and benediction, and perhaps a final pass by). The preferences of the clergy conducting the service will largely determine the order and content of the service.

When the visitation or funeral is to be held at the church, an open casket viewing is more likely to take place in the main auditorium rather than the vestibule of the church. There may also be options for the family to choose as to when to close the casket for the final time. Some may want to keep the casket open during the service, allowing for a final viewing after the service is over. Others may decide to close the casket for the service and re-open the casket for a final viewing at the conclusion of the funeral. Still others may want the casket closed before the service and left closed after that. Generally, the wishes of the family and the guidance of the clergy will determine the procedure to be followed.

In those instances where visitation is not held at the church prior to the funeral service, a processional into the church may be used. Since there are no acolytes or crucifers used in the Non-Liturgical Protestant churches, the clergy will lead the procession into the church, followed by the funeral professional, the casket and casket bearers, and the family. Additional funeral professionals may be included in the processional to assist the casket bearers with the casket and to ensure the proper seating of the family and casket bearers. Since many funeral services end with a final viewing by the family and friends, a recessional may not take place. If a recessional is held at the conclusion of the funeral service, it will follow the same order as the processional.

> **Basic Objectives of Funeral Service Professionals**
> **Objective 3**
>
> *"Appropriate Deference to Clergy/Officiants"*
>
> Deference is the quality of submitting to the judgment of a superior by the show of respect and reverence. The funeral professional mirrors the respect of the family for the individual they have chosen to lead them during their time of loss. These individuals are usually well trained, educated, and fill a prominent role in the survivors' lives. The funeral professional must understand this position and respect it, even they are of another faith or practice themselves. This respect will be reflected in the proper use of titles, both in public conversation and in print.

Although the order and the content of a Non-Liturgical Protestant service is difficult to define, it will most likely include an opening prayer, several musical selections interspersed through the service, scripture reading, a sermon, eulogy, and benediction or closing prayer.

The Committal Service

The committal service for Non-Liturgical Protestant denominations again will be dictated by the preferences of the officiating clergy, with input from the family. The procession to the grave site will be led by the clergy, with the casket, casket bearers, and family following. Once the casket has been placed on the lowering device and the casket bearers positioned, the clergy will typically lead those in attendance at the committal service through a prayer, scripture reading, and a benediction or closing prayer. The individual preferences of the clergy will determine whether or not they choose to make the symbolic sign of the cross on the casket with sand or flower petals, or do nothing in that regard at all.

If the final disposition is to be some method other than earth burial, the committal service may be held immediately following the funeral service omitting the processional to another site.

Dismissing the Visitation

Visitation is scheduled from 5pm to 8pm. It is now 9pm, and the family shows no sign of leaving. What do you do? Since turning out the lights or turning off the music is NOT an option, here is a suggestion. Around 8pm, ask the next of kin how they are doing. Upon gauging if they need more time, remind them that tomorrow will be a long day, and they should get some rest. Then invite them to participate in the "Casket Closing Ceremony."

Ask the family to join hands in front of the casket. If a minister is present, have him/her lead a prayer while you make preparations to close the casket. If a minister is not present, and the family is not comfortable with saying a prayer, you may lead them in the "Lord's Prayer." This prayer is usually long enough for you to properly close the casket. Remind the family that their loved one (call the deceased by name) will be in your firm's care, and if it is feasible they may return for a private moment prior to the funeral. Diplomacy is the key.

The Swiss Brethren Traditions:
Mennonite and Amish Funeral Rites

Introduction to the Mennonite and Amish Faith Communities

The Mennonite and Amish traditions have their foundation in many of the teachings and practices of the Protestant Reformation. These movements took hold primarily in German speaking countries across Western Europe. The term *Anabaptist* ("to baptize again") was a moniker attached to these believers by their detractors. Most Church historians separate these beliefs and practices as being part of the Radical Reformation rather than the Protestant Reformation. Where the Protestant Reformation was both a spiritual and political movement, the Radical Reformation was a strictly spiritual one. Many of the Protestant Reformers sought not only to reform the Roman Catholic Church, but also to set up State Churches to fill the political void. The Anabaptists believed in complete separation of Church and State, allowing freedom of worship and thought apart from any political entity.

Mennonite		Amish
The Mennonite family dates back to the Swiss Brethren who organized at Zurich, Switzerland, in 1525. The name *Mennonite* comes from the work and ministry of Menno Simons, who was an Anabaptist leader and author from 1536 to 1561. Their migration to America occurred in 1683 as a result of William Penn's offer of land and freedom of worship. There are still large populations of Mennonites in Pennsylvania, Ohio, Indiana, and Kansas, but they can be found on every continent.	or	The Amish family also dates back to the Swiss Brethren. The name *Amish* comes from Jacob Amman, who was part of a restoration movement within the Swiss Brethren. The resulting schism occurred in Europe in 1693. Their migration to America began in 1737. In 1749, one of their first leaders, Bishop Jacob Hertzler, arrived and settled in Northkill Creek, Pennsylvania. http://pabook.libraries.psu.edu/palitmap/AmishHistoryTimeline.html

It is interesting to note that the various circumstances causing schisms among the Mennonite communities have not carried over to the present day. In the American Colonies these groups developed and thrived alongside one another. It is a characteristic of their faith to promote their own beliefs without detracting from the beliefs of others.

For our purposes, we will categorize both the Mennonite and Amish traditions as Non-Liturgical Protestant. Necessary distinctions between the funeral practices of these two groups will be outlined on the following pages. However, it is up to the local funeral provider to ascertain the proper customs of the various groups he/she is privileged to serve as they will almost certainly vary, at least in part, from community to community.

The Mennonite Tradition

> "Simplicity and modesty in the selection of coffin and presence of flowers is liberating. By encouraging it and suggesting how to be simple and with dignity, the minister can free the bereaved from being intimidated by others' expectations and from trying to compensate for unresolved failures and alienations with outward show (*Minister's Manual*, page 188)."

Notification of the Clergy

Like most Non-Liturgical churches, the funeral professional is not required to ensure the minister has been notified. It is likely that the minister and faith community will already be aware of the death prior to the funeral home being contacted. In cases of lengthy illness, or prior to a surgical procedure, the family may ask for an anointing. This physical anointing has spiritual meaning to the participant. It is a time of repentance, and a reminder that God alone has the power to heal, no matter the external methods utilized.

Removal of Remains

There are no religious requirements or restrictions regarding the removal of the deceased. Only civil regulations will have an effect upon the removal procedure.

Preparation of the Remains

The Mennonite community permits embalming and cremation as a means of preparation and disposition. It is important to the faith community to have a service with the deceased present. When cremation is chosen, the service should be planned at an appropriate time to insure the cremated remains are present. "Since we are creatures of flesh and blood, most of us need visible and tangible actions to complete inner experiences. Therefore, the actions of grieving and giving thanks, of releasing the person who has died to God, are most complete when cremation occurs in time for the urn to be present for the funeral." (*Minister's Manual*, pages 187-188).

> **The Mennonite Funeral Service**
> **Suggested Order of Service**
>
> Silence or Music
> Hymn
> Scripture Sentences
> Greetings
> Opening Prayer
> Obituary
> Hymn
> Scripture
> Sermon
> Silence
> Remembrances by family and Friends
> Prayer of Thanksgiving and Petition
> Announcements
> Commendation
> Blessing of the Congregation
> Hymn

Dressing and Casketing of the Remains

Families are free to choose the casket and clothing for their loved one. These decisions will be based upon dignity and simplicity. The Mennonite faith encourages a mindset of moderation, simplicity, and modesty. These religious factors will act as an internal guide when making arrangements.

Pre-Service Considerations

The visitation will again follow traditional Non-Liturgical practices. Flowers are encouraged.

The Funeral Service

The elements of the service (listed) may be adapted to meet the family's needs. The religious service will focus on the comfort provided by a loving God and the hope the individual has in Christ. It also allows for the congregation to remember the impact the deceased had on their lives. This fits with the holistic view of salvation maintained by the Mennonite faith. God has wholly worked with the individual throughout life, and this life has had a Godly impact on humanity.

The Committal Service

The committal service will include Scripture sentences, a prayer, committal, and final blessing. In some communities a hymn may also be part of this final act of worship. In areas where it is permitted, the gathered community may choose to shovel some or all of the earth on the grave.

> **Swiss Brethren Heritage Religious Characteristics**
>
> Separation of Church and State
>
> Believer's Baptism (Opposite of Infant Baptism)
>
> Nonresistance (Refusal to take up arms)
>
> Nonconformity to the World

The Mennonite Traditions	
Classification	Non-Liturgical
Origin	radical reformation
	Anabaptist
	Swiss Brethren
	Menno Simons
Officiant	
Clergy Notification	not required
Removal	no restrictions
Preparation of Remains	no restrictions
Dressing and Casketing	no restrictions
Pre-Service	no restrictions
	no religious paraphernalia
	flowers permitted
The Funeral Service	
Place of Service	church or funeral home
Processional	optional
Rubric	none
Communion	none
Eulogy	permitted (remarks)
Flowers	accepted
Music	religious / dignified
Recessional	optional
The Committal Service	traditional
	may choose to shovel earth on casket if permitted

The Amish Tradition

Swiss Brethren Heritage

The Mennonite Church

Conservative Amish

Old Order Amish

Church of God in Christ

Old Order Mennonite

Reformed Mennonite

Mennonite Brethren Church

Mennonite Brethren in Christ

Defenseless Mennonites

General Conference of Mennonites

Hutterian Brethren

Krimmer Brueder Gemeinde

Notification of the Clergy

The ministry consists of Bishops or Elders, ministers who are pastors, or evangelists and deacons who take charge of congregations in the absence of the minister or Bishop. In most instances death will occur in a hospital or the deceased's residence. Due to strong family commitments, few deaths will occur in a nursing home. In most cases the family or experience with local customs will guide the funeral professional as to the appropriate time to notify the clergy.

Removal of Remains

There are no specific religious requirements or restrictions as to the removal of the deceased. The specific circumstances surrounding that particular death (length of illness, attending physician, and autopsy) will be civil factors affecting the removal of the remains.

Preparation of the Remains

There are no specific restrictions as to the preparation of the remains. For those families who wish, embalming is an acceptable method of preparation.

Dressing and Casketing of the Remains

The deceased may be dressed in white underwear and stockings and placed in a casket of the families' choosing. In some areas the "coffin"

style casket is still used, and may be locally crafted. If the deceased is a male, he may be dressed in a long gown, the top (or exposed) portion resembling a shirt with a pleat instead of buttons. An alternative choice of clothing is a white shirt, white trousers and a white vest. If the deceased is a female, she would be dressed in a long white gown and a white cape. In some areas, the sons may be responsible for dressing their father and the daughters for dressing their mother.

Pre-Service Considerations

Visitation for friends and neighbors may be held for one or two days prior to the service. Visitation and the funeral service may take place at the residence, especially in those groups

who worship in homes rather than church buildings. If the funeral is to be held at the church, a procession from the home to the church is traditional. With some groups, especially the Old Order Amish, the funeral procession will use a horse drawn hearse (or wagon), with the family and friends following in their horse drawn buggies.

The Funeral Service

The funeral service will most often take place in the church, or in the deceased's residence in those areas where no church exists. If the congregation is largely from a German background, the service may be conducted in German. Among the more conservative groups, the men will be seated separately from the women and children.

The Committal Service

Following the procession to the cemetery, either by automobile or horse drawn equipment, the coffin may be placed in a traditional outer enclosure for burial or, in some instances, a rough wooden box. After a simple committal service, the family and friends will return to the church or residence for a meal.

The Amish Tradition	
Classification	Non-Liturgical
Origin	radical reformation
	Anabaptist
	Swiss Brethren
	Jacob Amman
Officiant	
Clergy Notification	not required
	based on local tradition
Removal	no restrictions
Preparation of Remains	no restrictions
Dressing and Casketing	male — white shirt, trousers, and vest; alt., white gown in some areas / female — white gown and cape
Pre-Service	no restrictions
	no religious paraphernalia
	flowers permitted
The Funeral Service	
Place of Service	church, home, funeral home
Processional	none
Rubric	none
Communion	none
Eulogy	
Flowers	accepted
Music	religious / dignified
Recessional	none
The Committal Service	traditional

Glossary Chapter Two

AMISH: a conservative family-based group of Christians who broke away from the Mennonite community in 1720; sect noted for their strong family and community ties and separation from secular pursuits

ECUMENICAL: an epithet applied to a council regarded as representing the whole of Christendom

JACOB AMMAN: Anabaptist minister who broke away from the Swiss Brethren movement in 1693 over matters pertaining to excommunication; main writer and namesake for the Amish communities

MENNO SIMONS: ordained Roman Catholic Priest (1515), who converted to the Anabaptist cause and was baptized by immersion circa 1536; considered the namesake of the Mennonite movement

MENNONITE: Evangelical Christian community dating back to the 16th century, known for their rejection of infant baptism and opposition to war

NON LITURGICAL WORSHIP: *See also Scripture-Centered Worship*; form or order of worship having the scriptures as the central element, with the actual order of worship determined by the local congregation or clergy

PROTESTANT: any Western Christian who is not an adherent to the Roman Catholic Church

RADICAL REFORMATION: 16th century movement among German-speaking Christians which sought complete separation from Roman Catholicism's practices and doctrine

SWISS BRETHREN: first major group of Anabaptists which formed in Zurich in 1525; origin of many groups which hold to "believer's baptism"

Chapter 2 Review

1. What are the differences between Liturgical and Non-liturgical Protestant churches?
2. What is the origin of the Mennonite and Amish communities?
3. List the required clothing for Amish men and women.
4. Review special requirements for notification of clergy, removal of remains, preparation of remains, and dressing and casketing for each group included in this chapter.

Chapter 3
The Restoration Funeral Rite – Non-Liturgical

THE RESTORATION FUNERAL RITE

The following funeral traditions will focus on the subtle differences between the earliest Protestant groups and the Restoration groups which developed in America during the late 1800's. These groups did not develop in a vacuum, but on the foundations laid by the "Great Awakening." The following is an overview of the three movements which led to their establishment.

The First Great Awakening (1730-1740)

The "First Great Awakening" was a movement within Protestant (mainly Non-Liturgical) groups which focused on the concepts of devotion and a personal relationship with God. This movement stripped away remnants of sacramental theology which still remained after the Reformation. It rebelled against the deism and rationalism of the time. This movement affected established Christian communities in Europe as well as the American Colonies.

The Second Awakening (1790-1840)

Where the "First Awakening" was centered within established Christian communities, the "Second Awakening" was focused on the "unchurched." This was an American movement with a theological desire to set up Christ's kingdom on earth. The evangelical wing of the movement focused on proclamation of the Christian Gospel, while the social wing of the movement focused on correcting societal issues. Both groups succeeded to some extent. Churches experienced an influx of members and laid the foundation for social reform (Abolition, Prohibition, and Women's Suffrage). The evangelical and social aspects were the external portions of the movement. The internal portion of the movement found individuals who wanted to break away from established denominations in order to regain the primitive foundations of Christianity (see the section on The Church of Jesus Christ of Latter-day Saints).

The Third Awakening (1850-1900)

The "Third Awakening" moved past the theoretical stages of social reform and began to impact the social and political climate of American culture. The movement added the experiential element to Christian practice by focusing on the external work of the Holy Spirit in the life of adherents. This need for personal experience also added the need for personal and collective Bible studies (see also: Church of Christ, Scientist and Jehovah's Witnesses).

The Church of Christ, Scientist
Christian Science

Introduction to the Church of Christ, Scientist

The Church of Christ, Scientist is rooted in evangelical Protestant Christianity. Its followers are members of a religious movement that stresses spiritual healing. Christian Science is based on the teaching that God is wholly good and all-powerful, and that man is created by Him. Everything eternal, spiritual, and wholly good is called *reality*. Whatever is unlike God – injustice, sin, sickness, grief – is called *unreal*. The principle text, Science and Health with Key to the Scriptures, was written by Mary Baker Eddy in 1875 and contains the full statement of Christian Science beliefs. Mrs. Eddy founded the Church in Boston, Massachusetts, in 1879.

Brief History

1875 – Science and Health with Key to the Scriptures is published.

1879 – Individuals meet to develop a church based on the primitive (New Testament) model.

April 12, 1879 – Members vote to begin (reinstate) primitive Christian characteristics, including the lost element of healing.

June 1879 – The membership, 26 in number, voted Mary Baker Eddy to become their pastor.

1881 – Mary Baker Eddy is ordained.

Further Reading:
christianscience.com

Manual of the Mother Church: the First Church of Christ, Scientist, in Boston, Massachusetts, Mary Baker Eddy.

Included among the good and real is health, and among the unjust and unreal, disease. Because healing is brought about through spiritual understanding, members of the Church of Christ, Scientist normally do not seek medical help, including the use of hospitals and physicians. Death is viewed as one phase of the immortal existence of man.

> **Helpful Terms**
>
> *Reader/Practitioner*: individual permitted to lead in the lecture and Scripture reading
>
> *Mother Church*: the oldest original church from which other like-minded congregations have sprung
>
> *Rev. Mary Baker Eddy*: founder and teacher of the Church of Christ, Scientist
>
> <u>Science and Health with Key to the Scriptures</u>: published writing of Rev. Mary Baker Eddy in 1875; contains the full statement of Christian Science beliefs

Notification of the Clergy

The Church of Christ, Scientist has no clergy or ministers. The *Reader*, or *Practitioner*, may be the officiant of any service of the Church, including a funeral service. However, any member of the Mother Church (the original church in Boston) may serve as an officiant according to Church By-Laws.

Removal of Remains

Due to the members' beliefs toward sickness and healing, most deaths of Church of Christ, Scientists will come under the jurisdiction of a Coroner, Medical Examiner, or Justice of the Peace, and will take place somewhere other than a medical facility. The circumstances surrounding the death will determine whether or not any restrictions will be placed on the immediate removal of the remains.

Preparation of Remains

Embalming and public viewing are based on individual customs and wishes of the deceased and family. There are no beliefs within the Church to either encourage or discourage its members from being embalmed.

Dressing and Casketing of Remains

The clothing to be worn by the deceased and the casket to be used are left up to the individual preferences of the family. Because of its view toward death, and the fact that it is a church led by laymen, without clergy to express "official opinions," individual and family preferences determine most of the decisions involved when a death occurs.

The Funeral Service

Funerals for members of the Church of Christ, Scientist are similar to those of Non-Liturgical Protestant denominations, with a few notable exceptions. The funeral service itself may be held anywhere *except* the Christian Science Church. Most often this would be in the funeral home or the cemetery, either in a chapel or at the actual grave site. Since the officiant will be either a Practitioner or a Reader, the funeral professional should check with that person to determine the order of service.

The Committal Service

The method of disposition is again left up to individual preference. Earth burial, entombment, and cremation are all permissible.

The Church of Christ, Scientist	
Classification	Restoration, Non - Liturgical
Origin	Mary Baker Eddy
Text	<u>Science and Health with Key to the Scriptures</u>
Officiant	Reader / Practitioner
Clergy Notification	Not Required
Removal	No Restrictions Usually under Jurisdiction of Medical Examiner
Preparation of Remains	No Restrictions Interment, Entombment, Cremation
Dressing and Casketing	No Restrictions
Pre-Service	No Restrictions No Religious Paraphernalia Flowers Permitted
The Funeral Service	
Place of Service	Any Location *except* Church
Processional	None
Rubric	None
Communion	None
Eulogy	Family or Reader
Flowers	Accepted
Music	Religious / Dignified
Recessional	None
The Committal Service	Traditional

Avoid Confusion

Church of Christ, Scientist or *Christian Science*	*Churches of Christ*	*Scientology,* or *Church of Scientology*
founded in 1879 upon evangelical Protestant Christianity	autonomous Protestant Christian communities holding to similar practices and beliefs; many noted for weekly communion and lack of musical instruments	incorporated in 1952 (Camden, New Jersey) by L. Ron Hubbard; teaches spiritual rehabilitation through auditing

The Mormon Funeral Rite (LDS and RLDS)

Introduction of the Church of Jesus Christ of Latter-day Saints (Mormons)

Members of The Church of Jesus Christ of Latter-day Saints (LDS) consider the Church a restoration of true primitive Christianity, rather than a schism from established Protestant Christianity. The Church itself did suffer a schism following the martyrdom of Joseph Smith in Carthage, Illinois resulting in The Mormon Wars. In an effort to end the conflict, Brigham Young took pioneering families west to Utah and established a peaceful area to grow. The group that remained in the Midwest now refer to themselves as the Reformed Church of Jesus Christ of Latter-day Saints (RLDS). For our purposes, they will be considered jointly, as their funeral rites are virtually identical.

The nickname "Mormon" is associated with The Book of Mormon, which was translated by Joseph Smith. Mormons do not consider themselves to be a part of Protestant Christianity, but claim their authority directly from God. For our purposes, the Mormon Community is placed in the Non-Liturgical category based on the simplicity of their services and their lack of a strict rubric for worship. As of December 31, 2013, The Church of Jesus Christ of Latter-day Saints had 15,082,028 members in 29,253 Wards (www.lds.org/general-conference/2014/04/statistical-report).

Notification of the Clergy

Technically speaking, there are no full-time, professional clergy in the Latter-day Saints churches. Males 12 years or older can be ordained to the priesthood. Bishops, who hold full-time employment in areas outside of the church, are called from the priesthood to serve for an unspecified time and without compensation for their service to the Church. Since these individuals serve on behalf of the members, no funeral honorarium is expected, nor will it be accepted.

Brief History

September 1823 – Joseph Smith visited by Angel Moroni and told of the "Book of Mormon"

June 1829 – translation of the "Book of Mormon" completed

March 1830 – first printed copies of the "Book of Mormon" completed

July 1831 – Prophet Joseph Smith given site for the city of Zion (New Jerusalem) at Independence, Missouri

June 1844 – Joseph Smith martyred in Carthage, Illinois; Schism of the Church

February 1846 – majority of adherents move to Nauvoo, Nebraska (Winter Quarters)

April 1847 – Brigham Young begins journey to Utah

July 1847 – Brigham Young enters Salt Lake City

At the time of death, notification of the Bishop is not required by the Church. However, they should be notified prior to the time that services are finalized to avoid conflicting schedules.

Removal of Remains

There are no specific requirements or restrictions as to the removal from the place of death of a deceased member of the Latter-day Saints. Any restrictions or requirements would be due to civil rather than church laws.

Dressing and Casketing of Remains

There is no specific casket requirement for members of the Latter-day Saints. This is the choice of the family. The clothing to be used will depend on whether or not the deceased has completed the Temple Ordinance, or been *endowed*. For those members who have not been, the choice of clothing belongs to the family.

For a man who has been endowed, the clothing consists of the Temple garments, socks, shirt, trousers, tie, and moccasins. A robe is worn over the right shoulder extending diagonally across the chest in a straight line to the ankle, front and back. A green apron and white sash are placed over the robe at the waist. The sash is tied in a bow on the left side. A white cap is placed on the deceased's head before the casket is closed. The cap has a bow on the left side and string on the right side, which is tied to the robe.

For a woman who has been endowed, the clothing is similar. Temple garments, hose, slip, dress, and moccasins are placed on the deceased. The robe is worn over the right shoulder and extends diagonally across the chest in a straight line to the ankle. The apron and sash are placed over the waist and fastened similarly to those

> **Helpful Terms**
>
> *Bishop* – leader of the Ward; functions like a pastor in all aspects of the Ward and meeting house (chapel)
>
> *Ward* – geographical community of believers; may have familial, linguistic, or cultural characteristics
>
> *Temple Ordinance* – religious instruction, known as the endowment, given only in the Temple to those worthy members of the faith
>
> *Temple Garments* – special undergarments worn by members who have received the endowment in the Temple; function as a personal reminder of their devotion
>
> *Temple Clothing* – clothing worn by the endowed members of the Church at the Temple and for burial
>
> *Prelude* – music played prior to the service
>
> *Postlude* – music played after the dismissal of the service

Chapter 3: The Restoration Funeral Rite page 47

on the men. In addition, a white veil is draped on the pillow at the back of the head and placed over the face before the casket is closed. A ribbon is tied under the chin.

In most instances, members of the Latter-day Saints come to the funeral home to dress the deceased in the Temple clothing. Men commonly dress the men, and women dress the women. In cases where the endowed decedent cannot be dressed (tragic deaths or other issues), the Temple garments and Temple clothing are to be folded and placed next to the body of the deceased (https://www.lds.org/handbook/handbook-2-administering-the-church/meetings-in-the-church?lang=eng#18.6.4).

Pre-Service Considerations

The Bishop of the Ward should be contacted to determine the order of worship of the service. There may be some differences as to the order of worship based on the individual preferences of the officiant. Depending on the location of the funeral, which may be in the funeral home or ward chapel, determinations should be made as to the seating areas for the family and casket bearers, placement of the casket, and whether or not flowers will be present for the funeral service.

Visitation and viewing of the deceased is usually held the evening before the funeral service. This may take place at the funeral home, the residence, or elsewhere. If the funeral takes place at the ward chapel, it is possible the visitation will also occur there.

Order of Service

Family Prayer

Prelude

Opening Hymn

Invocation

Eulogy / Obituary

Musical Selection

Speaker(s)

Closing Remarks (Officiant)

Closing Hymn

Benediction

Postlude

The Funeral Service

Prior to the casket being taken to the main portion of the ward chapel or funeral home chapel, the officiant will lead the family in prayer. The Family Prayer is considered part of the overall funeral tradition, and is done with the deceased present. If the casket is already in the place where the service will be conducted, the guests will be dismissed prior to the Family Prayer. The funeral professional is present during this prayer and closes the casket after the time of devotion.

The funeral service may be held in the funeral home, ward chapel, or other location, but not in the Temple. Simplicity is the key word in the Mormon funeral. The use of the cross, crucifix, candles, and other such items are not permitted. Flowers are not discouraged, however, and in many communities of faith they are now encouraged and greatly appreciated. However, always keep the family's preferences in mind.

The Committal Service

While earth burial is the customary and preferred method of disposition following a Latter-day Saints funeral, other methods are also permitted. The preference of the family and the customs of the region may play a role in the decision as to the type of disposition.

The committal service is usually brief. The funeral professional escorts the casket to the grave and the guests are accommodated. The Bishop will have a few opening remarks, and a selected individual will dedicate the grave by offering a prayer and a blessing, if appropriate. Once this dedication is completed, the service is dismissed.

Basic Objectives of Funeral Service Professionals

Objective 4
"Dignity and Decorum"

Webster defines *dignity* as the state of being worthy, honored, or esteemed. *Decorum* is defined as propriety and good taste in conduct or appearance. For ease of understanding, dignity is the internal quality that motivates us, and decorum is the external quality of our service.

Funeral service is not a "job," it is a service, or in some areas a ministry. It relies on individuals who respect themselves and others. They treat the deceased, family, and community with great respect. Funeral professionals provide a safe environment for those in emotional and spiritual crisis. They function with an air of ease and professionalism, anticipating and preventing potential issues, and resolving known issues quickly. The goal is not to look as if we have done "this type of service" a hundred times before, but to understand the need and meaning of each service in which we are privileged to participate. The service, family, organization, or need of the moment is the utmost priority and should receive undivided attention.

The Church of Jesus Christ of Latter Day Saints	
Classification	Restoration, Non-Liturgical
Origin (Restorer)	Joseph Smith
Text	The Book of Mormon and Bible (KJV)
Officiant	Bishop
Clergy Notification	not required
Removal	no restrictions
Preparation of Remains	no restrictions interment, entombment, donation cremation (permitted)
Dressing and Casketing	endowed – temple garments and clothing; treated as sacred unendowed – family preferences
Pre-Service	proper religious music no religious paraphernalia flowers permitted
The Funeral Service	
Place of Service	LDS chapel (meeting house) / funeral home
Processional	follows family prayer
Rubric	None
Communion	None
Eulogy	family or bishop
Flowers	Accepted
Music	religious / dignified
Recessional	None
The Committal Service	dedication of the grave, and blessing, if applicable

The Jehovah's Witness Funeral Rite

Introduction to the Jehovah's Witnesses

For our purposes, the Jehovah's Witnesses will fall under the category of Restoration, Non-Liturgical churches. The adherents of the faith do not consider themselves Protestant or Catholic. They do not claim either tradition, but hold to a literal interpretation of Scripture which they believe has been misrepresented by both groups. The concept of Evangelical Christian will apply to members of this faith tradition.

As with many other religious groups, they are usually defined by their unique characteristics rather than their theological concepts. The two main characteristics usually discussed are their refusal to salute the flag of any country or to accept blood transfusions. These beliefs are based on literal interpretations of Scripture regarding issues of divine worship and obedience.

The overall structure of a Kingdom Hall is based on primitive Christianity and does not have a hierarchy. Elders will lead the congregation in study and worship. The organization does not have a centralized head where specific rules are set for the various congregations. Funeral service and disposition are usually based on individual conscience.

Notification of the Clergy / Removal of Remains

The Funeral professional will not be required to notify the Elder of the Kingdom prior to removal of remains. The only delay may be due to release by a hospital or medical examiner's office.

Preparation of Remains / Dressing and Casketing

If the family desires a visitation with viewing, embalming will be requested. There are no religious obligations regarding clothing or casket choice. The Jehovah's Witnesses also leave the decision of cremation up to each believer.

The Funeral Service / Committal Service

The service may take place at the funeral home or at the Kingdom Hall. It will be a religiously centered service, both in reading and music. Secular readings or songs will be prohibited by the

> **Helpful Terms**
>
> Elder – individual who acts as the officiant for the Jehovah's Witness funeral rite
>
> Kingdom Hall – proper name of the Jehovah's Witness worship facility

congregation. It will follow the characteristics of Non-Liturgical Protestant groups in that the service will be relatively simple and will not involve religious paraphernalia. The typical service will usually last thirty to forty minutes. The committal service will be led by the Elder and consist of Bible readings and simple commendation.

Jehovah's Witnesses	
Classification	Restoration, Non-Liturgical
Text	New World Translation of the Holy Scriptures
Officiant	Elder
Clergy Notification	not required
Removal	no restrictions
Preparation of Remains	no restrictions
Dressing and Casketing	no restrictions
Pre-Service	traditional visitation
The Funeral Service	
Place of Service	Kingdom Hall or funeral home chapel
Processional	None
Eulogy	member of the faith
Flowers	Accepted
Music	Congregational
Recessional	None
The Committal Service	dignified, graveside service

> **Increase Your Knowledge**
>
> To better understand your families who are of this faith, please visit http://www.jw.org.

Glossary Chapter Three

BISHOP: leader of the Ward; functions like a pastor in all aspects of the ward and meeting house (chapel)

ELDER: individual who acts as the officiant for the Jehovah's Witness funeral rite

ENDOWED: members of The Church of Jesus Christ of Latter Day Saints who have completed the Temple Ordinance

KINGDOM HALL: proper name for the Jehovah's Witness worship facility

MARY BAKER EDDY: founder, teacher, and writer of the Church of Christ, Scientist

MOTHER CHURCH: oldest original church from which other like-minded congregations have sprung

PRELUDE: music played prior to the service

POSTLUDE: music played after the dismissal of the service

READER/PRACTITIONER: individual permitted to lead in the lecture and Scripture reading in the Church of Christ, Scientist

SCIENCE AND HEALTH WITH A KEY TO THE SCRIPTURES: published writing of Rev. Mary Baker Eddy in 1875; contains the full statement of Christian Science beliefs

TEMPLE CLOTHING: clothing worn by the endowed members of the Mormon Church (both LDS and RLDS) at the Temple and for burial

TEMPLE GARMENTS: special undergarments worn by members of the Mormon Church (both LDS and RLDS) who have received the endowment in the Temple; function as a personal reminder of their devotion

TEMPLE ORDINANCE: religious instruction, known as the endowment, given only in the Temple to those worthy members of the faith in the Mormon Church (both LDS and RLDS)

THE BOOK OF MORMON: religious document translated by Joseph Smith; contains additional information regarding the person and works of Jesus Christ; used alongside the *Holy Bible* in the Mormon Church (both LDS and RLDS)

WARD: geographical community of believers; may have familial, linguistic, or cultural characteristics

Chapter 3 Review

1. Who is the founder of the Church of Christ, Scientist?
2. What is the main text for the Church of Christ, Scientist?
3. Where will a funeral not be held for the Church of Christ, Scientist?
4. Describe the burial garments for the deceased member of the Church of Jesus Christ of Latter Day Saints.
5. Who may participate in a Jehovah's Witness funeral?
6. Review special requirements for notification of clergy, removal of remains, preparation of remains, and dressing and casketing for each group included in this chapter.
7. Define the following terms:
    a. Reader
    b. Bishop
    c. Ward
    d. Temple ordinance
    e. Temple garments
    f. Temple clothing
    g. Elder
    h. Kingdom Hall

Chapter 4
The Roman Catholic Funeral Rite

The Roman Catholic Funeral Rite

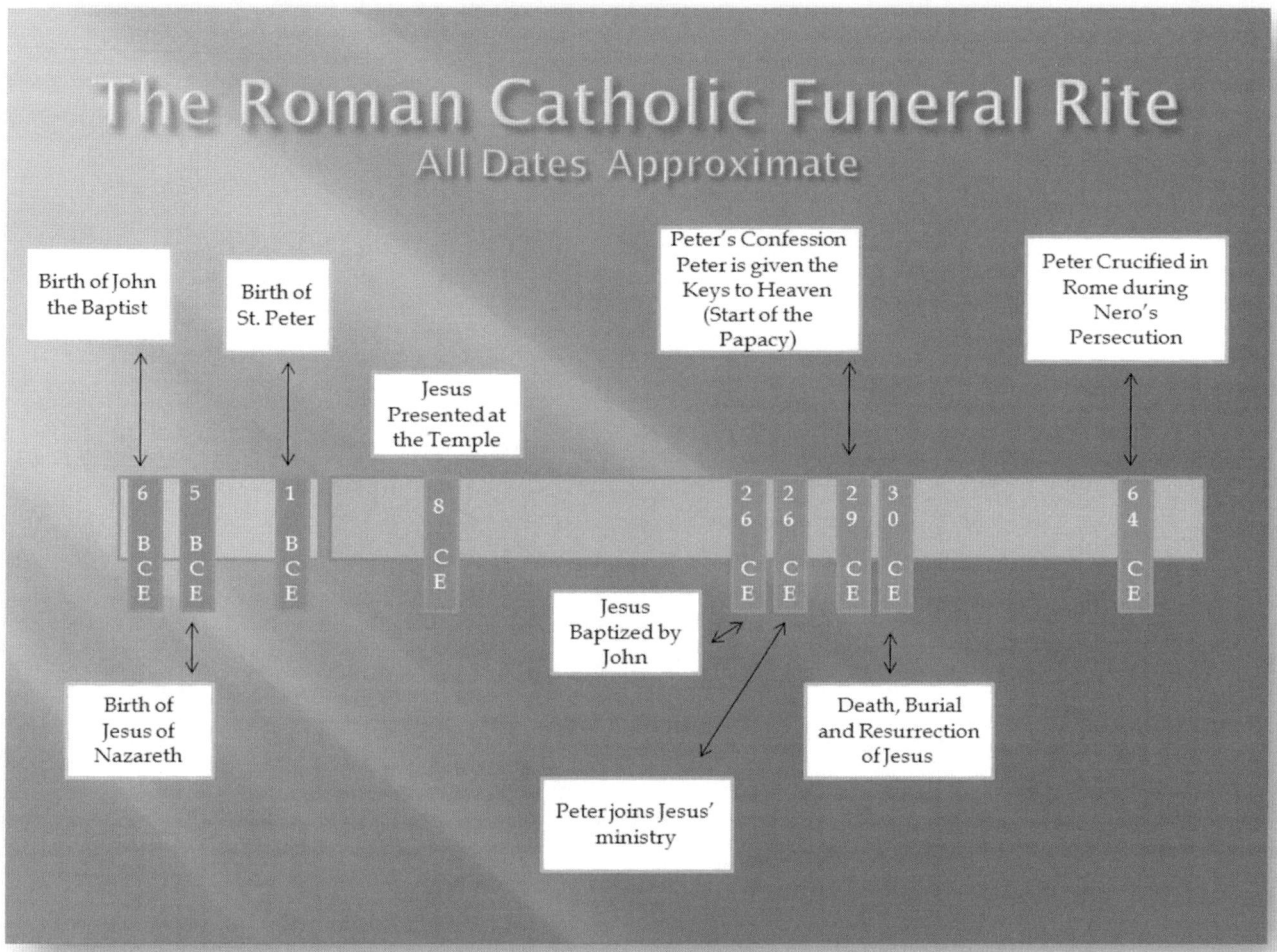

Introduction to the Roman Catholic Church

The Roman Catholic Church is the largest Christian organization in the world, with over one billion members worldwide. One source estimates the membership in the United States at 85 million (http://www.bbc.com/news/world-21443313).

The foundation of the Roman Catholic Church is based on the concept that Jesus Christ brought salvation to the world. Further, to continue His ministry, He developed an organization (the Roman Catholic Church) to carry on His work and teaching, and it now functions as a visible testimony of Christ's redemption. The Holy Spirit has preserved the teachings and attributes of Christian principles through the practice and Sacred Traditions[1] of the Church.

The Pope is the head of the Roman Catholic Church and the Bishop of Rome. The College of Cardinals serves directly under the Pope and takes care of the administrative duties of the Roman Catholic Church, as well as electing a new Pope when it becomes necessary. Archbishops serve as heads of archdioceses, which are geographical groupings of the many dioceses across the world. Individual Bishops then preside over a geographical grouping of the hundreds of parishes, with each parish being served by a Monsignor or Priest.

Church Office	Defined	Area of Influence	Area of Influence Defined
Pope	Head of the Roman Catholic Church and Bishop of Rome	Leader of the Roman Catholic Church (Universal)	
Cardinal	Dignity conferred upon Bishops or Priests making them princes of the Church	Assists the Pope Elects the Pope May be head of Archdiocese	Archdiocese – geological grouping of one or more dioceses under the jurisdiction of an Archbishop
Bishop	Head of a territorial unit of the Church	Head of a local diocese	Diocese – geographical grouping of parishes under the jurisdiction of a Bishop
Parish Priest	One ordained to carry out the works of the Church, subordinate to the Bishop; addressed as "Father"	Local parish	May be given the title Monsignor, an honorary title conferred upon a priest meaning "My Lord"

In regard to funeral rites, the Roman Catholic Church believes that all of its members should be buried from the Church with a Mass. There is no actual charge for being buried from the Church. The

---

[1] Sacred Tradition is a theological concept that encompasses the reservoir of all divine teaching. It is Sacred Tradition because it was given by Christ, through the Holy Spirit, and reveres Christ (Peter Kreef, 99).

funeral professional should be able to guide the family as to the practices regarding honorariums for the celebrant, cantor, or musicians.

The appropriate place to conduct a funeral service is in the local parish where individuals have received the Sacraments during their lifetime. Theologically, this belief is based on the words of St. Monica, the mother of St. Augustine. As she lay dying, she said to her son, "When I die, dispose of this body any way you wish. All that I ask of you is that you remember me at the altar of God."

Notification of the Clergy

The practice of notifying the deceased's clergyman when the death occurred was at one time a common and sensible practice. Today however, this practice can in no way be considered the usual practice. Factors such as the time of death, the place where the death occurred, and the relationship between the family and the clergy, each play a role in the family's decision as to the appropriate time to notify the clergy that the death as occurred.

For example, many families would hesitate to contact their clergy in the middle of the night purely for the purpose of stating that their family member had died. They might determine that more could be accomplished by waiting until morning when other decisions such as when and where to hold the funeral service could also be discussed. This might especially be true in those cases where the death was expected and where the Sacrament of the Sick had already been administered.

Since many priests want to participate in the decision making process for the date, time, and location of the funeral service, the funeral professional should determine whether or not the family has already contacted the priest who is to

> Sacrament of the Sick
>
> Anointing of the Sick
>
> The Sacrament of the Sick is one part of the final preparation for death. This final preparation consists of Penance, the Sacrament of the Sick, and the Eucharist when possible. These sacraments are preparing the individual to endure their suffering, as Christ endured his. They also serve as actions of faith, reminding the dying that the ultimate redemption (being with Christ) will be fulfilled at their time of death.
>
> "Penance, the Anointing of the Sick and the Eucharist as viaticum constitute at the end of Christian life "the sacraments that prepare for our heavenly homeland" (Kreef, pg. 374).

celebrate the Funeral Mass prior to entering into discussions which could lead to a decision concerning the scheduling of the Funeral Mass. A simple question during the initial contact with the family about whether the clergy has already been contacted will provide this answer, as well as lead the way to any additional discussion necessary in that area at the time.

Removal of the Remains

Generally speaking, there are no restrictions imposed by the faith which would prohibit the removal of the remains at the time of death. In those cases where the deceased was a member of the clergy or a religious order, there may be delays in making the removal should there be a desire for special prayers by members of the order prior to the removal.

Preparation of the Remains

There are no specific restrictions as to the preparation of the remains of laypersons. Religious articles worn by laypersons should be removed, recorded, and replaced after the preparation of the body. The family should then be asked if these religious articles are to be left on the body or removed and returned to the family prior to final disposition.

Dressing and Casketing the Remains

A deceased layperson should be dressed in clothing selected by the family. Members of the clergy will be dressed in the robes of the station of their priesthood. Members of religious orders should also be attired in the robes of their position. In some religious communities, the role of dressing and casketing the clergy or members of a religious order may be the responsibility of designated members of the specific order.

Religious objects may be placed in the hands as requested by the family or Church officials. The rosary beads are most commonly used, and are usually placed in the deceased's hands. A crucifix, sacred heart, or other objects of religious significance may be placed in the head panel or foot panel, on or near the casket.

The Visitation Set-Up

The funeral home should have the needed religious paraphernalia necessary for the Roman Catholic visitation. There are three main elements necessary for the presentation. A free standing *crucifix* should be centered behind the casket. The *prie dieu* will be placed immediately in front of the casket, just to the right of center. This allows the community to pray for the deceased and still have room for viewing. Some individuals lead the congregation in the saying of the Rosary from the *prie dieu*. *Vigil lights* will be placed at the head and foot of the casket.

The Wake

A wake will usually be held in the funeral home, family home, or Church the evening before the Funeral Mass. The wake may include the saying of the Rosary or a prayer service. The purpose of the wake is to provide the family and community a time of devotion. It is meant to offer a time of reflection on the meaning of life, death, and eternal life. At this time prayer cards are made available to the guests. It is also appropriate to have Mass Cards available for those who wish to request a special Mass on behalf of the deceased.

The service may be led by a priest, deacon, layperson, member of the family, or even the funeral professional. If a priest is to lead the service, the time should be set only after direct communications have been made with the priest. This service is normally scheduled by the family, and approved by the Church during the funeral arrangements conference.

The priest is free to substitute various Scripture readings based on the circumstances. The people in attendance may recite portions of the prayers (responses). In some cases the priest or deacon may conduct the whole service. The wake service is not meant to replace the Funeral Mass.

Helpful Terms

Scapular: a piece of cloth or a medal with religious significance usually worn around the neck

Rosary Beads: beads and a crucifix used as an aid in the recitation of prayers

Crucifix: a cross with a figure or image representing the body of Christ (Corpus Christi) on it

Sacred Heart: in the Roman Catholic faith, a religious picture, usually of Jesus Christ

Prie Dieu: a kneeling rail

Vigil Lights: in the Roman Catholic faith, a set of two candles, one placed at the head of the casket and one placed at the foot of the casket during the visitation period in the home or funeral home

Prayer Cards: card with name of decedent and prayer or verse; may or may not include dates of birth and death

Mass Cards (Spiritual Bouquet): document indicating offering of a mass for a specific intention

Pre-Mass Considerations

The Funeral Mass will normally take place at the church. There are several options which may determine the activities of the funeral home staff, family, and guests attending the Funeral Mass. In some areas, it is customary for the family and friends to meet at the funeral home prior to departing for the church. If the family wishes, someone may lead a prayer before or after the final viewing. If a priest is in attendance, he may lead the prayers. At the appropriate time, the funeral professional may announce the departure to the church and dismiss the friends, allowing them to pay their last respects before moving outside to their automobiles. After the friends have gone, the family can then be given time for a final, private farewell. After the family returns to their automobiles, the funeral home staff can close the casket, placing the crucifix on top of the casket head panel, and then prepare to move in procession to the church.

In some areas the local parish will permit the final viewing at their location, usually in a private room or in the narthex. If this is the case, the casket is closed prior to the entrance rite.

If the family does not plan on meeting at the funeral home prior to the Funeral Mass, the funeral home staff will normally arrive at the church shortly before the Mass is scheduled to begin.

The Funeral Mass

The Funeral Mass actually begins when the casket is ready for transition from the narthex into the nave of the church. The casket bearers and family members accompany the casket into the narthex to await the celebrant and the altar attendants. The procession to meet the body is led by the crucifer and two altar attendants, one who carries the Holy Water and one who carries the incense. The celebrant is last in the procession (see: Entrance Rite).

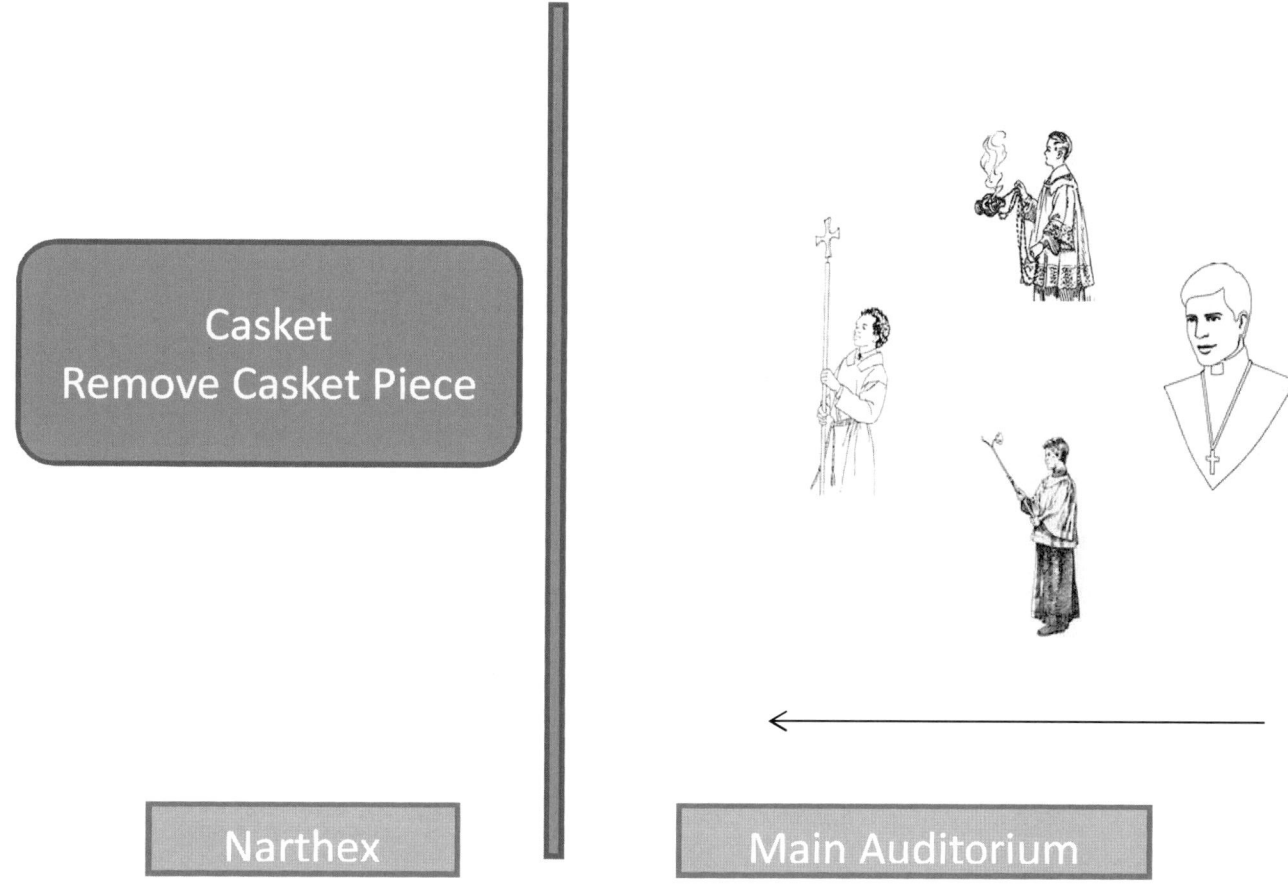

If a casket piece covers the casket, it is removed at this time and set aside. If the casket is covered with a United States flag, determination should be made during the funeral arrangements conference whether the U.S. flag or the pall is to be used. NOTE: If a pall is to be used, the flag should be folded and set aside. Following the greeting and invocation, the celebrant conducts the blessing of the casket with Holy Water, symbolizing the individual's initial baptism into the Roman Catholic Church. After this blessing, the family or funeral professional will place the pall on the casket.[2] *The Order of Christian Funerals* permits the placing of a crucifix, the gospels, or a Bible on the pall as a representation of Christian faith and practice.

The processional down the aisle of the church is led by the crucifer, followed by the altar attendants and the priest. Depending upon the width of the aisle, the casket bearers may proceed

---

[2] "A reminder of the baptismal garment of the deceased, the pall is a sign of the Christian dignity of the person. The use of the pall also signifies that all are equal in the eyes of God." (James 2: 1-9) Order of Christian Funerals 10.

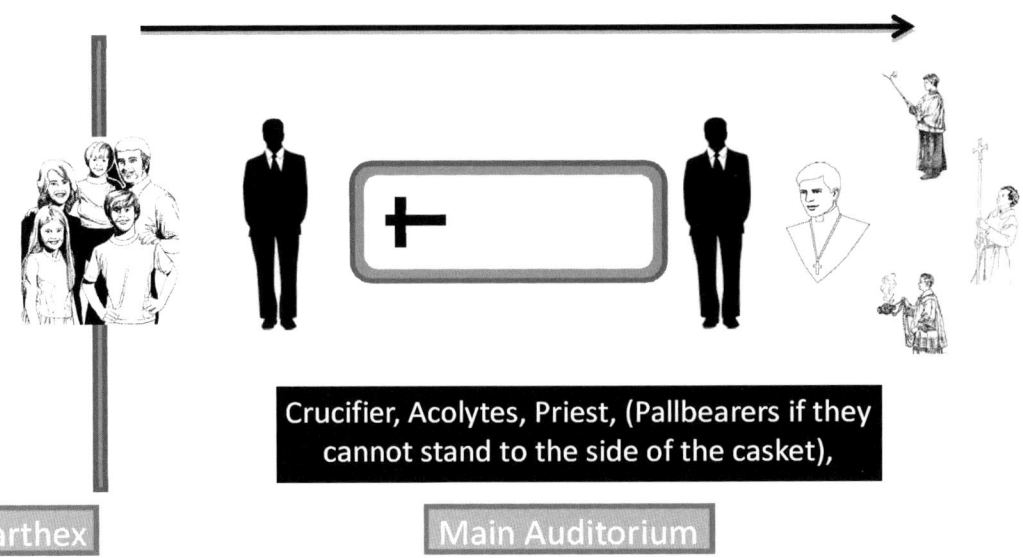

alongside the casket, or if the aisle is too narrow, they may move ahead of the casket immediately following the priest. The family will follow the casket down the aisle.

When the procession reaches the foot of the altar, the celebrant will proceed up the steps to the chancel while the funeral professional seats the family and casket bearers according to the pre-determined customs of that particular parish. The casket should be placed at right angles to the altar. Deceased laypersons and nuns are placed with their feet toward the altar and paschal candle, while deceased priests are placed with their head toward the altar. After the bearers and family are positioned, it is customary for the funeral professional to pay his/her respects by bowing or genuflecting toward the altar. After this symbol of respect and reverence, the funeral professional will exit via the side aisles.

After the funeral professional's exit from the nave, the celebrant will conduct several Bible readings, consisting of the Psalms and the Gospel. A homily will then be

> **Helpful Terms**
>
> *Narthex*: the vestibule; entryway to the church
>
> *Nave*: the seating section of the main body of the church
>
> *Pall*: a symbolic cloth covering placed over the casket in the vestibule of the church
>
> *Chancel*: the area around the altar of the church, usually enclosing the clergy and other officials
>
> *Altar*: an elevated place or structure on which sacrifices are offered or at which religious rites are performed
>
> *Paschal Candle*: a candle placed near the casket during the Funeral Mass that signifies the everlasting light of Christ
>
> *Genuflect*: the act of bending the knee as an indication of reverence or as an act of humility
>
> *Communion*: reception of the Eucharist
>
> *Final Commendation*: the ending portion of the Funeral Mass

said by the celebrant. (This may also include a eulogy to be said by the celebrant, a family member, or friend.) Following this portion of the Mass, the celebrant will partake of and offer Communion. The family and other members of the Roman Catholic faith may participate. Those who are not of the Roman Catholic tradition are typically invited to come forward and receive a blessing from the Church. The desire to participate in this way is indicated by approaching the priest and crossing the arms over the chest.

Following this sacrament, the celebrant will descend from the chancel to say the Final Commendation, again blessing the casket with incense and Holy Water. After this blessing, the funeral professional will return to the front of the church for the recessional.

The Recessional

As the celebrant moves toward the crucifer, the funeral professionals will return to each end of the casket. If room permits, the casket is turned, forming the sign of the cross. The casket is once again placed in the center of the aisle. As the recessional makes its way out of the church, the same order as the processional will be followed.

At the narthex the white pall is removed from the casket and placed at the back of the church. As the casket exits, the priest makes the sign of the cross. The aspersion is eliminated at this point because it was used at the meeting of the body at the door of the church. The incensation was given at the offertory.

Variations of the Funeral Mass are common, and it is the responsibility of the funeral professional to maintain constant contact with the clergy to avoid confusion and ensure a seamless service.

The Committal Service

If final disposition is to be interment (earth burial), the sexton or another cemetery

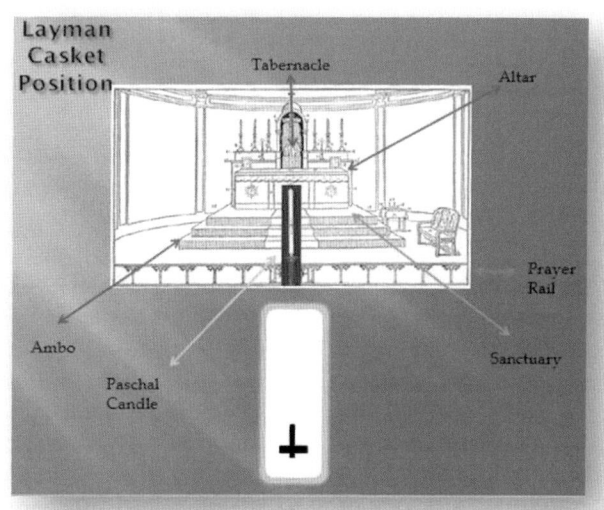

employee will generally lead the procession to the gravesite, insuring the correct placement of the casket on the lowering device and assisting with the placement, if needed. The priest will lead the casket which is either carried by the casket bearers or moved on a mechanical device with the casket bearers walking alongside. The family and friends will follow the casket to the gravesite and gather around the casket for the committal service.

The committal service consists of a Psalm, scripture reading, invocations, and prayer reflecting the reunion of the deceased with Christ forever. There is less emphasis on the element of sorrow and more on the true joy that death brings to the deceased. The committal service also stresses the fact that for the survivors this loss is only for a short period of time with the promise of a Heavenly reunion later.

At the conclusion of the farewell, the crucifix may be removed from the casket to be given to the family. In some areas, the priest will bless the crucifix before giving it to the family.

Guidelines for Cremation

The Church, through the centuries, has followed the practice of burial or entombment after the manner of Christ's own burial/entombment both out of respect for the human body and faith in the resurrection. It is still the expressed will of the Church that this hallowed and traditional practice be maintained. However, recognizing particular circumstances and varying cultures and customs in different parts of the world, the Roman Catholic Church issued an instruction in 1963 on cremation which allows some latitude under certain conditions for those Roman Catholics who request their bodies be cremated.

It is evident that the Church no longer prohibits cremation, as long as cremation is not chosen out of any anti-Christian motive or antagonism. However, because the Church will allow cremation does not mean that the Church has no exceptions as to how cremation will fit into the scheme of the Roman Catholic Funeral Liturgy.

Because of the structure of the Roman Catholic liturgy and the long-standing tradition of honoring the body of the deceased, the Church prefers that cremation is a process that takes place after the Funeral Mass and final commendation. Cremated remains must be either buried or inurned. Scattering of cremated remains or possession of cremated remains at the home is strongly discouraged.

There are always exceptions to every rule or guideline, but the norm for Roman Catholics who choose cremation over burial or entombment is to follow the scheme set out in the "Order of Christian Funerals."

1. Wake service (with the body present)
2. Funeral Mass (with the body present)
3. Final Commendation to take place at:
    a. Cemetery, for earth burial
    b. Mausoleum, for entombment
    c. Cemetery, for cremation
    d. Church, for cremation
    e. Crematory chapel, for cremation

When cremation is chosen there is a fourth step beyond the final commendation. The cremated remains are to be buried, entombed, or inurned in consecrated ground or columbarium. Under no circumstances are they to be left with the funeral home or crematory, taken home, or scattered. They are to be given the dignity of a Christian burial. Should cremation take place prior to funeralization, the cremated remains should be present for the Funeral Mass.

> **Addressing the Priest as *Father***
>
> See Matthew 23:9 – This passage has been one of conflict between the Roman Catholic Church and some Protestant denominations. The Catholic Church believes there is one "Father," which is "God, the Father." When the term is applied to a Priest, it is not acknowledgement of deity, but of leadership and guidance. Elisha called Elijah his father, as a spiritual guide. St. Paul referred to Timothy as his son in the ministry. Paul was Timothy's spiritual help. This same concept is accepted by the Roman Catholic Church and its parishioners. In a sense, ordained ministers act as kind parents assisting their flock (children) to grow in their faith.

"Although cremation is now permitted by the [Roman Catholic] Church, it does not enjoy the same value as burial of the Body. The Church clearly prefers and urges that the body of the deceased be present for the funeral rites …" (Decree on Cremation by the NACCB, August 15, 1997; page 391 in The Order of Christian Funerals with Cremation Rite).

The Roman Catholic Church	
Classification	liturgical
Origin (Restorer)	Jesus Christ / St. Peter
Officiant	priest
Clergy Notification	prior to establishing service time and place
Removal	no restrictions
Preparation of Remains	layperson – no restrictions; holy orders – potential individual restrictions; cremation permitted
Dressing and Casketing	laypersons – no restrictions; holy orders – vestments (may dress own members) ministers – vestments; holy objects optional
Pre-Service	set-up to include: prie dieu, vigil candles, crucifix, hand-held or visual aids to the faith (rosary beads, scapular, sacred heart, individual crucifix, etc.), prayer cards, spiritual bouquets
The Funeral Service	
Place of Service	church or sanctified location for mass
Processional	crucifer, acolytes, priest
Rubric	Order of Christian Funerals
Communion	prior to final commendation
Eulogy	priest's decision; may be after mass, prior to final commendation
Flowers	church preference
Music	church preference
Recessional	same as processional
The Committal Service	processional, scriptures, prayer, dirt or flower petals placed on casket, crucifix blessed and presented to next of kin

Turning the Casket

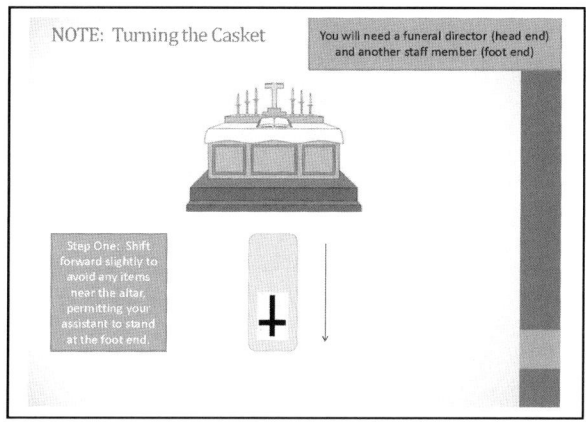
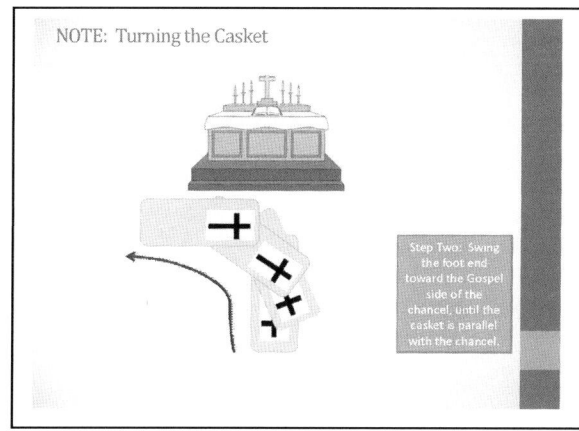
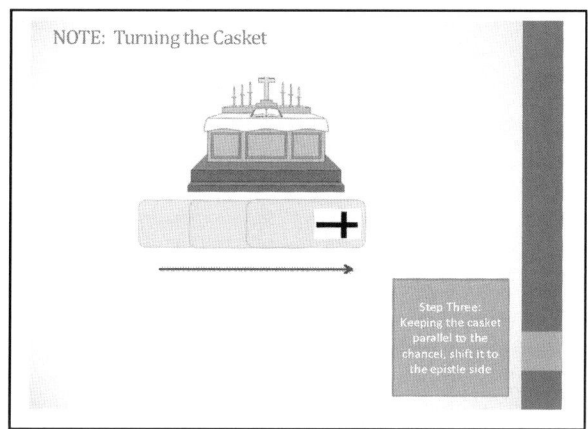
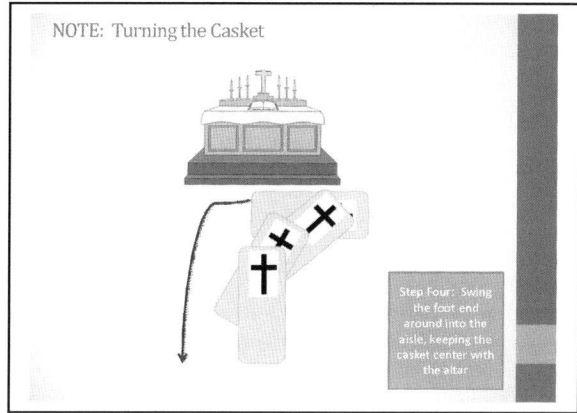
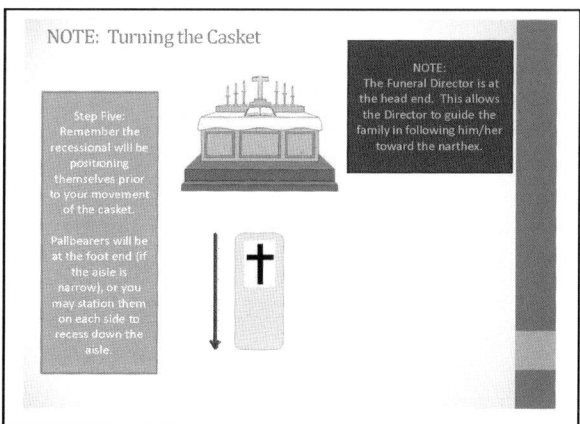

Glossary of Roman Catholic Terms

ACOLYTE: altar server at the Mass; altar attendant

ALTAR: elevated place or structure on which sacrifices are offered or at which religious rites are performed; in the Christian faith, a table on which the Eucharist or Holy Communion is offered

ARCHBISHOP: head of the Archdiocese

ARCHDIOCESE: geographical grouping of one or more dioceses under the jurisdiction of an Archbishop

BISHOP: head of a territorial unit of The Church

BOW: inclination of the body made while standing during liturgical prayer

BROTHER: in the Roman Catholic faith, a man who is a member of a religious order without being ordained or while preparing for ordination

CANTOR: Precentor; leads congregational responsorial hymns and psalms

CARDINAL: dignity conferred upon Bishops or Priests making them princes of the Roman Catholic Church

CASKET BEARER (Pallbearer): one who actively bears or carries the casket during the funeral service and the committal service

CELEBRANT: officiant who celebrates the Mass in the Roman Catholic Church

CHANCEL: area around the altar of the church, usually enclosing the clergy and other officials; one of two main areas of the church, the other being the nave

CHAPEL: building or designated area of a building in which services are conducted; may contain an altar

CHRISTIAN BURIAL CERTIFICATE (Christian Burial Permit, Priest Lines): letter or form from a priest stating the eligibility of the deceased for funeral rites according to the laws of The Roman Catholic Church

COMMUNION: reception of the Eucharist (body and blood of Christ)

CROSS: religious emblem consisting of two plain bars which intersect at right angles to each other

CROSS BEARER: one who carries the cross in a religious procession

CRUCIFER: one who carries the crucifix in a religious procession

CRUCIFIX: cross with a figure or image representing the body of Christ (Corpus Christi) on it

DEACON: in the Roman Catholic faith, a member of the clerical order (clergy) just below a Priest

DIOCESE: geographical grouping of parishes under the jurisdiction of a Bishop

Ecclesiastic: of the church or clergy

Entrance Rite: approach of the celebrant and his assistants to public worship

Epistle side: right side of the church as the congregation faces the altar; contains the lectern from which the Old Testament and Epistle Lessons are read

Eucharist: body and blood of Christ (consecrated elements of Holy Communion)

Eucharistic Minister: layperson assigned to provide Holy Communion, after the elements have been blessed by a priest

Final Commendation: ending portion of the Funeral Mass

Funeral Liturgy (Funeral Mass): name of the funeral service in the Roman Catholic Church; formerly called the Mass of Christian Burial

Genuflect: act of bending the knee as an indication of reverence or an act of humility

Gospel Side: left side of the church as the congregation faces the altar; place for the reading of the Gospels and delivery of the homily by the minister

Holy Water: consecrated (blessed) water

Homily, sermon: preaching of the Word of God by the clergy

Host: consecrated bread of the Eucharist

IHS: first three letters in the Greek word for Jesus

Incense: mixture of various resins burned to produce a pleasant odor; used in Church rituals

INRI: abbreviation for the Latin term meaning "Jesus of Nazareth, King of Jews"

Kiss of Peace: mutual embrace

Liturgical Worship (Eucharist Centered): prescribed order or form of worship specific to a particular denomination which will have the Eucharist or Holy Communion as its central element

Mass: liturgical celebration of the Eucharist in the Roman Catholic Church

Mass Card (Spiritual Bouquet): document indicating the offering of a Mass for a specific intention

Monsignor: honorary title conferred upon a Priest

Narthex (Lobby, Vestibule, Foyer): vestibule or entry way to the church

Nave: seating section of the main body of the church; one of two main areas of the church, the other being the chancel

Obsequies: antiquated term for funeral rites or funeral services

Officiant: individual who leads in the funeral service

Pall: symbolic cloth covering placed over the casket in the vestibule of the church, signifying that in the eyes of God all people are created equal

Pallbearer (Casket Bearer): one who actively bears or carries the casket during the funeral service and the committal service

Paschal Candle: in the Roman Catholic faith, a candle placed near the casket during the Funeral Mass that signifies the everlasting light of Christ

Pope: head of the Roman Catholic Church and Bishop of Rome

Prie Dieu (Prayer, Kneeler): kneeling rail for prayer

Priest: one ordained to carry out the works of the Church, subordinate to the Bishop; addressed as "Father"

Procession/Processional: organized, predetermined method of moving from the narthex to the altar at the beginning of the funeral service

Recession/Recessional: organized, predetermined method of moving from the alter to the narthex at the end of the funeral service

Related Rites: generally celebrated by the family of the deceased together with the Roman Catholic minister; usually performed during critical moments of the grieving journey; include Prayer After Death, Gathering in the Presence of the Body, and Transfer of the Body to the Church or Place of Committal

Requiem Candles: three candles placed on each side of the casket in the front of the altar; recently replaced by use of the Paschal Candle in many areas of the country

Rite: a form of liturgy regulated by tradition and law

Rite of Committal: celebrated prior to the Funeral Liturgy, usually at the funeral home on the morning of the Funeral Liturgy, preceding the closing of the casket; recited by family, friends, minister, priest, or funeral professional; may also be combined with the Rite of Final Commendation when necessary adoptions are made

Rosary Beads: beads and a crucifix used as an aid in the recitation of prayers

Rosary Prayers: series of prayers consisting of the "Lord's Prayer," "Ava Maria," and "Glory Be to the Father"

Rubrics: in Liturgical churches, stated directions in a prayer book or liturgical manual regarding the order of service as approved by the denomination

Sacrament of the Sick: part of the final preparations for those who are seriously ill or in danger of losing their lives; usually done via anointing the individual with oil

Sacred Heart: in the Roman Catholic faith, a religious picture, usually of Jesus Christ

Sacristy: room adjacent to the chancel in which the liturgical vessels, utensils and vestments are kept and where the clergy vest

Sanctuary: the part of the chancel containing the altar

Scapular: piece of cloth or a medal with religious significance, usually worn around the neck

Sign of the Cross: sign made with the right hand touching the forehead, breast, left shoulder, and right shoulder, successively

Spiritual Bouquet: document indicating the offering of a Mass for a specific intention

Tabernacle: shrine in which the Blessed Sacrament (elements of the Eucharist) are kept

Thurible: receptacle in which incense is burned

Thurifer: altar attendant who carries the thurible

Transepts: wings of the main part of the church which may serve as small chapels for baptisms, weddings, and even small funeral services

Vestments: ritual garments worn by the clergy

Vigil for the Deceased: formerly called the Wake or Rosary Service; a public prayer, focusing on the proclamation of God's Word; may be said in the funeral home, residence, or church, depending on where the visitation is taking place

Vigil Lights: in the Roman Catholic faith, a set of two candles, one placed at the head of the casket and one placed at the foot of the casket during the visitation period in the home or funeral home

Wake: historically, a watch kept over the deceased; an all-night vigil

Other, Related Terms

ABLUTION, ABLUERE (*LAT.*): rinsing of the mouth, Eucharistic vessels, and fingers after touching the sacred host

ABSOLUTION: sacramental remission of sin

ACCLAMATION: people's response in Liturgical worship

AGNUS DEI (*LAT.*): lit., *Lamb of God*

ALB, TUNICA ALBA: white undergarments of linen, reaching to the feet

ALLELUIA: lit., *Praise ye God*

AMBO: raised place between the sanctuary and nave for reading of the lessons / sermons

AMEN: lit., *So be it* or *let it happen*

AMICE: shoulder cloth; rectangular lined cloth with straps (30" X 20") worn under the alb

APSE, APSIS: semicircle end of the presbytery

ASPERGES: act of sprinkling the congregation with Holy Water prior to Sunday Mass

BRANDEUN: cloth that has been laid upon the grave of a saint, then used as a substitute for a relic

BREAKING OF BREAD: fractioning of the altar-breads before communion

BURIAL: earth interment

BURIAL GROUNDS: see Cemetery; an area of ground set aside and dedicated for the final disposition of dead human bodies

CASSOCK, ALB: garment reaching the ankles; black worn by Priests (white in the tropics), purple worn by Bishops, red worn by Cardinals, and white worn by the Pope

CEMETERY: see Burial Grounds; an area of ground set aside and dedicated for the final disposition of dead human bodies

CEREMONIES: sacred public worship

CHALICE, CALIX: vessel in which wine is consecrated at Mass; composed of the cuppa (cup), nodus (stem), and the base (foot)

CHANT: singing or intoning of all liturgical portions of a service

CHASUBLE, CASUAL: outer garments worn by a Priest during a Mass

Chrism: mixture of olive oil and balsam, blessed by a Bishop, and used in the administration of certain sacraments

Christian Wake: prayer service

Commentator, precentor: layperson who leads prayer and/or reads Scripture

Communion Chant: chant that accompanies the distribution of communion

Communion Paten: flat plate held under the chin at communion

Concelebration: corporate celebration of the same Mass by several priests

Consecrated ground: ground set aside for a special purpose, blessed by the clergy

Cope: semi-circle cloak reaching the feet and provided with a hood

Corporial: cloth upon which the Eucharist is placed

Crypt: chamber or vault; chamber in a mausoleum, of sufficient size, generally used to contain the casketed remains of a deceased person

Dalmatic: Deacon's vestment

Exequies: Liturgy of the dead

Gospel: *lit.*, "good tidings"; when pluralized, refers to the first four books of the New Testament (Matthew, Mark, Luke and John)

Lector: individual who reads out the Scriptures

Libera: last responsorial prayers after the Mass

Maniple: strip-like vestment worn on the forearm of sub-deacons

Mass for the Dead: term for a mass that is celebrated for a deceased person when the body is not present in the church

Mother Superior: position held by a woman in charge of a convent of women

Nun (Sister): in the Roman Catholic faith, a woman who is a member of a religious order, especially one bound by vows of poverty, chastity, and obedience

Oils: consecrated oils used in liturgical anointing

Paten: dish or plate for the host during communion

Purificator: small cloth for the chalice used during communion

Pyx: vessel or cabinet in which the Blessed Sacrament is kept

Veil Chalice: square cloth, usually of the same material as the chasuble, used to cover the chalice at Mass

Chapter 4 Review

1. Roman Catholic hierarchy includes the Pope, Bishops, and priests. Discuss their respective areas of influence.
2. Explain the Sacrament of the Sick.
3. Describe the necessary equipment for the Roman Catholic visitation.
4. May non-Roman Catholics participate in the funeral service?
5. Describe the order of the processional.
6. What are the Roman Catholic guidelines for cremation?
7. Review special requirements for notification of clergy, removal of remains, preparation of remains, and dressing and casketing for each group included in this chapter.
8. Define the following terms:
    a. Scapular
    b. Rosary beads
    c. Crucifix
    d. Sacred heart
    e. Prayer cards
    f. Mass cards
    g. Altar
    h. Pascal candle
    i. Final commendation

Chapter 5
The Eastern Orthodox Funeral Rite

The Orthodox (Christian) Funeral Rite

Church of Constantinople Established by Andrew

Church of Antioch Established by Thomas

Church of Rome Established by Peter

Church of Jerusalem Established day of Pentecost

Church of Alexandria Established by Mark

See of the Roman Catholic Church

Sees of the Orthodox Church

Background

The early Christian communities often looked to established regional churches as guides of faith and practice. These churches were considered equals, and would often send emissaries to discuss theological concepts and practices (Church Counsels). The five main Sees of early Christianity were located at Jerusalem, Rome, Antioch, Alexandria, and Constantinople. The leaders of these churches acted as equals and saw the Jerusalem Church as the First Among Equals.

> **Eastern Orthodox Church Communities**
>
> Egyptian (Coptic) Church
>
> Syrian Orthodox Church and Mar Thoma Syrian Church (Sometimes referred to as Oriental Orthodox)
>
> Greek Orthodox Traditions: Greek, Russian, Albanian, Hungarian, American, etc.

Assyrian Orthodox Communities

The first division occurred after the First Council of Ephesus in 431. The Nestorian Controversy was focused on Nestorious who studied at the School of Antioch. His opponent was Cyril of Alexandria. The main issues were the dual nature of Christ (divine and human) and the proper view of Mary (*Theotokos* or *Christotokos*). The Church of Antioch, along with the regional churches, separated from the established Christian community. Today this tradition continues with the Assyrian Orthodox Church. These traditions can been seen in the United States with the communities of the Mar Thoma Syrian Church www.marthomanae.org, and The Syrian Orthodox Church in North America www.syrianorthodoxchurch.org.

Egyptian (Coptic) Communities

Twenty years after the Nestorian Controversy, another issue regarding the divine and human natures of Christ would arise at the Council of Chalcedon. The situation once again deteriorated causing the emissaries from Alexandria to side with the Greek writings of Cyril against the Latin delegates from the West. The Coptic Church would separate from the remaining Christian Communities in 451. Today the Church of Alexandria is the Mother Church for Egypt and all of Africa. According to www.coptic.org there are approximately 93 Coptic churches in the United States. While many of these fall under the jurisdiction of Alexandria, there are two dioceses in the United States. Visit www.suscopts.org and www.lacopts.org to learn more about these organizations.

Helpful Terms

Orthodox: right belief or right worship.

Sees: The seat (sedes) of episcopal or religious authority

Theotokos: Greek term meaning "Mother of God"; preferred title of Mary for the Roman Catholic tradition and Orthodox Communities after 431

Christotokos: Greek meaning "Mother of Christ", preferred title for Mary in the Oriental Orthodox tradition

Filioque: Latin for "from the Son"; the Latin view (Roman Catholic and Protestant) is that the Holy Spirit proceeds from both the Father and the Son; the Greek view (Orthodox) is that the Holy Ghost proceeds from the Father only.

Icon: holy pictures, usually of Christ, the Mother of Christ, and the Saints, found covering the walls, iconostasis, and special shrines around the church

Iconostasis: a solid screen, covered with icons, at the front of the church, dividing the sanctuary from the body of the building (nave)

The Constantinople Communities

The final division between the early Church traditions happened in 1054. The main issues involved the use of icons, the *filioque* controversy, and Rome's claim of Primacy. The Greek speaking Eastern Church of Constantinople and the Latin speaking Roman Catholic Church finally parted ways.

The Constantinople or Byzantine communities are the most recognizable Orthodox Churches today. These churches grew throughout Eastern and Southern Europe. Their families are broken down by regional and linguistic differences. Orthodox churches have large numbers of adherents in Greece, Hungary, Albania, Belarus, Romania, and Russia, just to name a few.

The American Orthodox community springs directly from the Russian Orthodox Church. The Russian community began in Alaska, prior to the purchase of this territory by The United States. Originally called The Russian Orthodox Greek Catholic Church of North America, the Church was granted autocephaly and entered into communion with the Moscow Patriarchate in 1970. For more information see http://oca.org/history-archives/oca-history-intro.

The Orthodox Funeral Rite

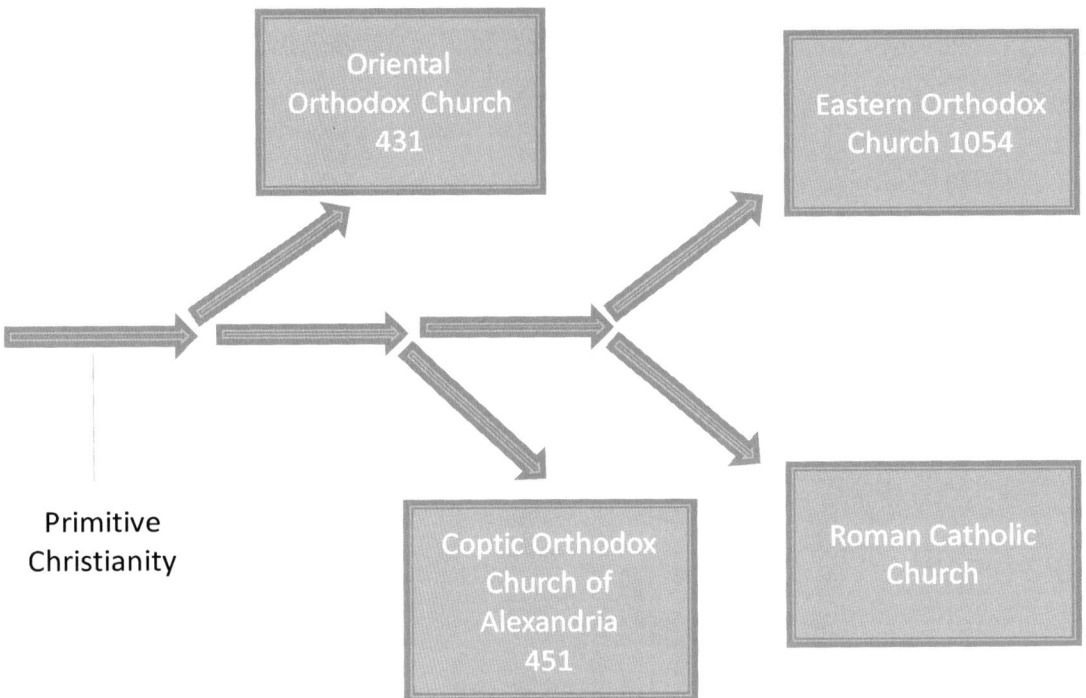

Introduction to the Orthodox Church

The Orthodox Church is a family of independent, flexible, auto-cephalous (self-governing) churches. Unlike the Roman Catholic Church, headed by the Pope, each Orthodox Church is governed by an independent Council of Bishops, called a synod. For the most part, these churches agree on doctrinal matters and members are free to participate in the ritual of communion in any Orthodox church.

The word Orthodoxy has a double meaning of "right belief" and "right worship." The Orthodox Church holds that they teach and practice the proper means of glorifying God.

> The Orthodox Church can almost certainly lay claim to having the most titles by which it is can be called. It is frequently named according to the location or make-up of its members, as in:
>
> *Greek Orthodox Church*
>
> *Russian Orthodox Church*
>
> *The American Orthodox Church*
>
> *The Eastern Orthodox Church*
>
> *Orthodox Catholic Church*

According to the 2010 Census of Orthodox Christian Churches in the USA, there are over one million forty-four thousand adherents in the United States. "The American Orthodox Christians worship in 2,380 local Orthodox parishes which belong to 20 different National Orthodox Church bodies including 6 Oriental Orthodox Churches" (www.acrod.org/news/releases/2010-census).

Notification of the Clergy

Unlike the Roman Catholic Church and some Protestant practices, the Orthodox communities do not practice "last rites." The Church does not require the funeral professional to notify the clergy at the time of death.

Removal of the Remains

There are no religious restrictions concerning the removal of the deceased. The removal staff will be able to remove the remains upon obtaining the necessary releases. Only civil law will dictate any delays in the removal procedure. Members of the Orthodox community utilize the concept of "fallen asleep in the Lord" to describe the deceased.

Preparation of the Remains

The practice of embalming is accepted and encouraged for funeral service. Since there is public viewing and final anointing of the body, the practice of embalming is necessary for the community.

Helpful Terms

Cantor: a person who accompanies the priest in chanting hymns pertaining to the liturgical service

Funeral service: the proper name given to the Orthodox Church service conducted for the dead

Icon: holy pictures, usually of Christ, the Mother of Christ and the Saints, found covering the walls, iconostasis, and special shrines around the church

Iconostasis: a solid screen, covered with icons, at the front of the church, dividing the sanctuary from the body of the building

Solea: the open area before the altar in an Orthodox Church

Taper: a wax candle lit in the narthex of the Orthodox Church, signifying prayers and petitions being offered up to God

Trisagion: three short services or blessings conducted at the funeral home the evening before the funeral service, on the day of the funeral service before leaving the funeral home for the church, and at the cemetery following the funeral service

Dressing and Casketing the Remains

While the European custom is to shroud the body, in the United States the deceased is usually dressed in clothing chosen by the family. The casket used will also be chosen by the family based upon their desires.

Pre-Service Considerations

The visitation, historical Parastasis, begins with the Trisagion. It is usually held in the funeral home the evening before the funeral service and again the following day immediately prior to the funeral service. Since this service is usually held in the funeral home, the funeral professional should determine what religious equipment will be necessary. Normally candles will be placed at each end of the casket, a cross behind the casket, and an icon at the foot end of the casket.

The Funeral Service

The final Trisagion may be held at the funeral home or at the church. The members of the family and pallbearers will often be the only ones in attendance at this service. The service will be very short, often lasting only five or ten minutes. When the Trisagion is held at the funeral home, the participants will usually go in procession from there to the church.

> **Using Terminology**
>
> The *Panachida* is the rubric for the funeral service. It is a pamphlet containing the *Small Panachida*, which is for the vigil service at the funeral home, and the *Great Panachida*, the service held at the church. It also includes the interment service.
>
> The *Trisagion* are the prayers that are part of the *Small Panachida* and *Great Panachida*.
>
> The *Parastasis* is the "watch" or "all-night vigil" over the lifeless body.

When the procession arrives at the church, the casket and family will move into the church where they will be met by the priest. The priest will bless the casket with holy water before leading the procession

---

Chapter 5: The Eastern Orthodox Funeral Rite page 83

down the aisle of the church. A cantor may accompany the priest during the processional.

The casket is led feet-first down the aisle and placed in the Solea with the foot end of the casket nearest the altar. The casket is usually left open during the funeral service. The service will follow a liturgical order with readings, prayers, and hymns from a special book titled the *Panachida* (the Byzantine Rite is available as Panachida: The Office of Christian Burial). The final portion of the service may include a eulogy.

After the eulogy, the casket is turned so that it is parallel to the Iconostasis (the portion extending across the front of the church). The priest anoints the body with earth or sand and olive oil. An icon is placed at the foot end of the casket and those seated on the right side of the church may pass the casket, stopping to kiss the icon (Ceremony of the Last Kissing) on their way. The icon is then moved to the head end of the casket and those seated on the left side of the church may stop and kiss the icon before passing by the casket. After the final viewing and kissing of the icon, the friends exit the church and return to their automobiles. The family then has an opportunity for the final viewing before the casket is closed.

Although there are always exceptions, some guidelines which are generally followed with Orthodox funerals include holding the funeral service in the church, and not having

---

Order of the Funeral Service
from
http://www.goarch.org/ourfaith/ourfaith9218

The Funeral Service of the Eastern Orthodox Church consists of hymns, prayers, and readings from the Scriptures. The order of the Service is as follows:

The Trisagion Service, chanted at the funeral home or in the church on the evening before the funeral service and on the day of the funeral, at the graveside following the funeral service, and for memorial services.

Selection of verses from Psalm 119 (LXX 118) in three stanzas: Part I – verses 1, 20, 28, 36, 53, and 63; Part II – verses 73, 83, 94, 102, 112, and 126; Part III – verses 132, 141, 149, 161, 175, and 176.

Blessings (Evlogetaria): "Blessed are You, O Lord, teach me Your statutes!" (Psalm 119:12)

Kontakion and Hymns in each of the Eight Tones

Scripture Readings: (a) 1 Thessalonians 4:13-18 and (b) John 5:24-30

Small Litany, Prayers, and Dismissal

The Kiss of Peace and the anointing of the body

The chanting of the Trisagion Service at the cemetery

funerals on Sundays and certain Holy Days recognized by the Orthodox Church. The use of flowers is generally permitted although this will vary from church to church, as will the number of flowers permitted in the church for the funeral. As is true with all religions/denominations, the funeral professional should visit with church officials before there is a need to determine the preferences for that particular group.

The Orthodox View of Cremation

Cremation is considered objectionable in the Orthodox Church. "As a matter of principle, the incineration of the bodies of Orthodox Christians in crematoria is not permitted, in view of the fact that this custom has been introduced by atheists and enemies of the Church. In all individual, extenuating circumstances, the decision is left to the diocesan bishop" (http://orthodoxinfo.com/death/cremation.aspx).

The Committal Service

Disposition usually involves earth burial or entombment. Upon arriving at the cemetery for the committal service the priest will lead the casket in procession to the burial site, accompanied by the cantor, if possible. The committal service will include a litany of readings and prayers by the priest and cantor. A closing prayer signals the end of the committal service.

Information Topics	General Information
Classification	liturgical
Origin	Jesus Christ
Leadership	pope: spiritual leader of the mother church and those churches who are in communion; bishops, parish priests, deacons
Clergy Notification	not required
Removal	no restrictions
Preparation of Remains	interment or entombment; cremation objectionable
Dressing and Casketing	clergy / religious orders – vestments; parishioners – no restrictions
Visitation / Wake Parastas	small Panachida, free standing cross, vigil lights, icon, flowers permitted
The Funeral Service	
Place of Service	church encouraged for funeral
Religious Items	Icon
Processional	priest and cantor lead procession
Rubric	*Panachida*
Communion	none
Eulogy	permitted
Flowers	permitted
Music	congregational / cantor
Recessional	same as processional
The Committal Service	committal service at place of disposition with the Trisagion

Glossary of Orthodox Terms

CANTOR: a person who accompanies the priest in chanting hymns pertaining to the liturgical service

DEVINE LITURGY: eucharistic celebration in the Eastern Orthodox communities of faith

FUNERAL SERVICE: the proper name given to the Orthodox Church service conducted for the dead

GREAT PANACHIDA (PARASTAS) – Office of Christian Burial in the [Greek Orthodox] Church

ICON: holy pictures found covering the walls, iconostasis, and special shrines around the church

ICONOSTASIS: a solid screen, covered with icons, at the front of the church, dividing the sanctuary from the nave

PANACHIDA: rubric for the funeral service; a pamphlet containing the *Small Panachida*, for the vigil service at the funeral home, and the *Great Panachida*, the service held at the church; also includes the interment service

PARASTASIS: "watch" or "all-night vigil" over the lifeless body

SOLEA: open area before the altar in the Orthodox Church

TAPER: a wax candle lit in the narthex of the Orthodox Church, signifying prayers and petitions being offered up to God

TRISAGION: three short services or blessings, conducted at the funeral home the evening before the funeral, prior to leaving for the church, and at the cemetery

Chapter 5 Review

1. What is The Orthodox Church's view of cremation?
2. Describe The Ceremony of the Last Kissing.
3. Review special requirements for notification of clergy, removal of remains, preparation of remains, and dressing and casketing for each group included in this chapter.
4. Define the following terms:
    a. Orthodoxy
    b. Icon
    c. Iconostasis
    d. Solea
    e. Trisagion

Chapter 6
The Jewish Funeral Rite

The Jewish Funeral Rite

Introduction to Judaism

Judaism, thought to date back to the 16th century B.C.E., was the first monotheistic religion. Founded by Abraham, Judaism was the foundation for both Christianity and Islam. Judaism is based on the doctrine of one God and ancient scriptures, namely the *Old Testament* and the *Talmud* (oral teachings of the *Torah*).

The Three Religious Jewish Groups in the United States

Orthodox	*Conservative*	*Reformed*
Continue the ancient traditions and beliefs	Still follow the ancient traditions, but have accepted gradual changes as a natural growth of the religion	Allow greater flexibility and have adapted to modern practices

While there are many common customs, traditions, and beliefs among the Orthodox, Reform, and Conservative Jews, there are also some significant differences in their practices of worship and lifestyle. The same is true of their funeral customs and practices. This text will first examine Orthodox Jews, the most fundamental in their practice. The Reformed and Conservative groups, while not identical, follow many of the same funeral practices, and will be combined for our purposes here. The funeral professional should be well aware of the various congregations in his or her community and the practices that they follow.

> **FUN FACTS**
>
> The *Torah* may also be called the *Five Books of Moses*, or the *Pentateuch*.
>
> It is composed of the first five books of the Bible's Old Testament: Genesis, Exodus, Leviticus, Numbers, and Deuteronomy.
>
> It is also the first section of the *Tanakh*, the Hebrew Old Testament.

The Orthodox Jewish Funeral Rite

Notification of the Rabbi

All services and arrangements are under direct supervision of the local rabbi and the funeral professional. The rabbi should be immediately notified unless death occurs on the Sabbath, in which case the rabbi should be notified immediately after the end of the Sabbath. The group leader of the *chevra kadisha* should also be notified.

> **Helpful Terms**
>
> *Rabbi*: a teacher or ordained leader in the Jewish faith
>
> *Sabbath/Shabbat*: the Jewish Holy Day, beginning at sundown Friday and ending sundown Saturday
>
> *Chevra kadisha*: Hebrew meaning "Burial Society"; holy brotherhood of men or women from a synagogue who care for the dead (often referred to as "washers" by laymen)

Removal of the Remains

No removals are to be made on the Sabbath, unless death occurs in a public place and/or if the remains interfere with public health. If death was from a violent cause, all bloodstained clothing and other material should be removed with the remains and placed in the casket with the remains. This is done in order to return the entire body back to the elements from which it was created.

With the death of an Orthodox Jew, the role of the chevra kadisha begins when death has been definitely established. Straw is placed on the floor, then covered with a sheet. Members of the chevra kadisha carefully undress the remains, men handling men and women handling women, before carefully positioning the body on the sheet face up with feet facing the door. The windows in the room are to be opened.

The deceased is addressed by name in Hebrew and is asked by the participants to forgive any indignity. While the deceased is being positioned, prayers are recited. The limbs are straightened, the eyes are closed, and the mouth and jaw may be tied with a handkerchief or piece of cloth. A block or pillow is placed under the head, and a candle is lit and placed at the head of the deceased. All mirrors within the household are covered. The total proceedings are referred to as Laying Down (*hashkava*). Only observant Jews may handle the body. The body

> **Why cover the mirrors?**
>
> Go look at yourself in the mirror. In the image you see characteristics of your grandparents, parents, siblings, and children. These images will add to your sorrow. This tradition allows the faithful to experience the grief of the loss, without adding to overwhelming sorrow.

should be covered at all times and handled with dignity and respect. If it is not possible to perform the *Hashkava* at the time of death, it need not be done before the *Taharah*.

There are many variations in accordance with geographical and individual communities. Local rabbis should be contacted individually by the funeral professional in order to determine the preferred customs of that particular community.

From the time of death until the time of the funeral, a *shomer* (watchman; plural, *shomrim*) will remain either in the room with the body or within visual distance. Psalms and traditional prayers for the departed are recited by the shomer in the presence of the deceased. Smoking, eating, and unnecessary conversation are forbidden in the room with the body. Men and women may serve in the capacity of shomer for any deceased person. If the body is being maintained prior to taharah under refrigeration, the shomer should be able to see the door of the unit. These proceedings are referred to as "The Watch" (*shmira*).

Preparation of the Remains

If civil laws require embalming, these laws supersede the laws and regulations of the synagogue. Otherwise, there is no embalming. If the body is embalmed, the blood is placed in containers and placed in the casket along with the body. For those

> **Helpful Terms**
>
> *Hashkava*: a prayer for the "laying down" of deceased relatives
>
> *Taharah*: the ceremonial washing of the deceased by the chevra kadisha before burial; serves as a ritual purification or cleansing of the body
>
> *Taharah Room*: a room set aside in a mortuary or funeral home for the practice of the taharah; may be utilized for both Jewish and Islamic body preparations
>
> *Aron*: Hebrew term meaning "container"; a casket made entirely of wood and containing no metal parts or animal glues
>
> *Shomer*: the watcher (sitter) who remains with the body until burial
>
> *Shmira*: "The Watch"; the period of time the shomer is with the deceased

who have died in a tragic manner, any bloodstained clothing and any cloths used to clean the blood should be placed in the casket with the deceased.

Normal preparation of the Orthodox Jewish body begins with the rite of washing the deceased by the chevra kadisha as directed by the rabbinic authority. The chevra kadisha is made up of the respective sex of the deceased. Prior to the taharah, the leader will acquire the necessary sundries to complete the task. The Tahara Room should be supplied in advance with the following: *tachrichim* (traditional burial clothing) for men and women, broken pottery, soil from Israel, wooden instruments, pails and pitchers, new cloth strips for washing, and a *tallit* (prayer shawl) for men. In the event the deceased dies from a communicable disease, those performing the tahara may wear protective garments and rubber gloves. If a coffin or casket (*aron*) is used, it is to be a plain wooden pegged box without ornaments or lining, and containing no metal parts or animal glues. Holes may be bored in the bottom to allow the deceased to be closer to the earth.

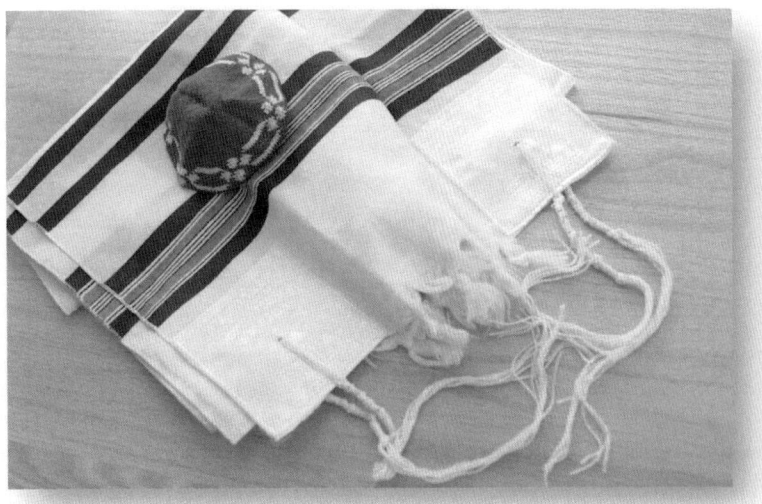

Dressing and Casketing the Remains

The chevra kadisha shrouds the body. The tachrichim should be made of white linen without binding, hems, knots, or pockets. The tachrichim for men consist of seven garments. There are eight garments in a woman's tachrichim.

Men's Garments	Description
Mitznefes	a headdress
Michnasayim	trousers with closed feet
K'sones	a shirt with sleeves
Kittel	a robe with collar and sleeves
Avnet, Gartel	a sash
Tallis	a prayer shawl
Sovev	a small linen bag used as a headrest

Women's Garments	Description
Bonnet	covering for the head
Michnasayim	trousers with closed feet
K'sones	a shirt with sleeves (blouse)
Kittel	a robe with collar and sleeves
Avnet, Gartel	a sash
Apron	
Face Cover	
Sovev	a small linen bag used as a headrest

The sovev is a linen bag filled with straw and soil from Israel which is placed in the casket as a headrest. Israeli soil is also spread on the floor of the casket. After the body has been carefully placed in the casket, personal articles may be included. Any clothing or jewelry on the body at the time of death should also be placed in the casket. Once this is done, the casket is closed and generally will not be reopened. The casket is then removed from the area of preparation, moving feet first to the place of burial.

Orthodox Jews will wash their hands prior to re-entering their residences after being in contact with, or in the same room as, the remains.

Pre-Service Considerations

Most Orthodox Jewish funerals are held in the funeral home or at the cemetery; very few are held in the synagogue. If the funeral is to be held at the funeral home, the aron is placed parallel to the front of the chapel or stateroom and covered with a pall. A menorah is placed nearby. Flowers are not normally used in an Orthodox Jewish funeral. However, since there may be some individuals who are not familiar with the family's customs, there may be times when flowers will be sent to the funeral home. The funeral professional should determine with the family and rabbi how best to handle this issue, should it arise.

The Funeral Service

The order of the service is determined by the rabbi. No funerals may be held on the Sabbath. A cantor will often accompany the rabbi and take part in the funeral service, usually chanting or singing the readings. In many areas, the funeral home will provide transportation for both the rabbi and cantor.

The Funeral Procession

The cortege (*levaya*) may stop at the synagogue. If this occurs, the funeral professional should escort the rabbi to the synagogue door. The rabbi will recite a prayer as the funeral professional opens the doors of the funeral coach. This provides one last contact for the deceased with the synagogue. Once the prayer is over, the funeral professional should close the door of the funeral coach and escort the rabbi back to his automobile. The cortege will then proceed to the cemetery.

The Committal Service

In a traditional service, during the procession to the grave the rabbi will stop the casketbearers seven times to pray and recite a psalm (frequently Psalm 91). There is usually a symbolic pause before continuing after each of these stops. Once the aron reaches the grave, the casketbearers place the casket on wooden planks or cloth straps over the newly dug grave in the Jewish cemetery or the Jewish section of a cemetery. The site around the actual grave is usually unadorned, with no artificial grass, mechanical lowering device, or tent.

The final prayers are recited by the rabbi, and the family and friends recite the *kaddish*. The clothing of the family may be cut or torn at this point in the committal service. The casket is then lowered into the ground. The rabbi reluctantly shovels earth onto the casket and then lays the shovel down or plants it into the earth to be picked up by members of the family, who will also shovel dirt onto the casket until the casket is covered. The shovel is not passed from person to person in order to avoid passing along ones grief to another mourner.

Upon leaving the gravesite, the mourners will wash their hands three times by pouring water on them from a vessel, beginning with the right hand. Their hands are then air-dried.

Basic Objectives of Funeral Service Personnel
Objective 5

"Smoothness of Procedure"

Plan:

The number of funeral service personnel should be planned in advance. Location, family needs, religious contacts, and estimated number of attendees should be considered. This decision should never be made the day of service, especially just moments prior to the service. It should be considered during the arrangement conference. Funeral staff should be assigned specific responsibilities to ensure all areas of service are provided. Staff members should know how they will be contributing to the overall service.

Practice:

It is difficult to find time in the funeral home schedule to hold "mock" services. Paperwork, aftercare, at-need families, and services take up most of the day. However, having a walk-through with the staff will provide discipline and continuity in serving families. This is especially helpful in keeping the staff aware of service types that the firm may not serve on a frequent basis.

Perform:

Do the service as it has been planned and practiced. But service does not end at the final committal. It ends when everyone involved has had opportunity to evaluate what went well identify opportunities for future improvement.

Plan, Practice, Perform

NOTE: It is extremely important to remember that a number of variations of the Orthodox Jewish funeral rite exist, dependent upon who the deceased was, the timing of the death, distance to be traveled before burial, etc. This material should be used only as a guide. *Consulting your local rabbinic authority is of the utmost importance!*

Laws of Mourning

Upon the death of a member of the Jewish faith, blood relatives are to observe certain specified mourning periods. During these periods, the relatives are to humble themselves as a display of respect for the deceased. Although they may rend (tear) their garments either on the day of the death or at the committal site, this custom is frequently replaced with the wearing of a torn ribbon on the clothing. Mourners are also expected to refrain from work, festivities, or amusements during this time. The mourning periods listed below may apply to the Orthodox, Reform, or Conservative Jewish faiths.

Name	Time of Mourning
Shiva (7 days)	The observance of shiva begins on the day of the burial and ends on the seventh day after burial. During this time, mourners do not shower or bathe, wear leather of any kind, or shave. Mirrors remain covered. Seating is low – stools or low benches – to symbolize being brought low by mourning. No mourning is to take place on the Sabbath, but it does count as one of the seven days of shiva.
Sholoshim (30 days)	The thirty days immediately following burial are a mourning period during which mourners abstain from all festivities or amusement following the death of a relative. Men do not shave or cut their hair for this period as well.
Shneim asar chodesh (12 months)	Those mourning the loss of a parent face an additional period of mourning lasting eleven months from the end of sholoshim. Sons are to recite the kaddish as part of synagogue services. Most activities return to normal, but there remains a restriction on attending festive occasions and large gatherings, especially if live music will be present.
Yahrzeit (1 year)	The anniversary date of a death is called a yahrzeit. A yahrzeit candle is burned in the home for a twenty-four hour period.

The Conservative and Reformed Jewish Funeral Rite

Differences Between Orthodox and Conservative / Reformed Communities

It is important for the funeral professional to realize that Conservative and Reformed Jewish communities have the freedom to choose between following the Orthodox funeral customs completely, only in part, or not at all. Since each community will be unique in their preferences and customs, the funeral professional should become acquainted with the group(s) in his/her community prior to meeting with a family. Remember that these differences may encompass everything from casket selection to preparation and disposition of remains and service type.

Glossary of Jewish Terms

Aron: Hebrew word meaning container; a casket made entirely of wood, containing no mental parts

Cantor: religious singer who assists the clergy – the rabbi in the Jewish faith, or the priest in the Eastern Orthodox faith

Chevrah Kadisha: Hebrew phrase meaning *Holy Society*; group of men or women from the synagogue who care for the dead; may be referred to by laymen as *Washers*; in the past, took care of all funeral arrangements and preparation for Jewish funerals

El Malei Rachamin: in the Jewish faith, a memorial service; literally *God full of compassion*; usually the last prayer of the funeral service; sometimes referred to as the *Malei*

Hesped: in the Jewish faith, a eulogy or true evaluation of the deceased's life as a part of the funeral service

Judaism: monotheistic religion of the Jewish people

Kaddish: in the Jewish faith, prayer recited for the deceased by the direct mourners (parents, siblings, spouse, and children) for the first time at the conclusion of the interment service; subsequently recited by children for parents at every service for eleven months and by other categories of mourners for 30 days

Kevurah: in the Jewish faith, the burial

Kriah: Hebrew word meaning *rending or tearing*; symbol of grief; tear in the upper corner of the garment or on the symbolic ribbon worn by survivors

Levaya: in the Jewish faith, the funeral procession

Menorah: in the Jewish faith, a candelabrum with a central stem bearing seven candles; oldest symbol in Judaism

Mogen David (Star of David): in the Jewish faith, a hexagram formed by the combination of two triangles; also called the Jewish Star; symbolizes a new hope for the Jewish people

Rabbi: teacher or ordained leader in the Jewish faith

Shabbat: Jewish Sabbath; begins at sundown Friday and ends at sundown Saturday

Shivah: in the Jewish faith, a seven-day mourning period

Sholoshim: meaning *30* in the Jewish faith; 30-day mourning period

Shomer: in the Jewish faith, a watcher; one who sits with the body until burial

Synagogue: Orthodox Jewish religious building

Tachrichim: hand-sewn white linen shroud in which deceased members of the Jewish faith are dressed

Taharah: in the Jewish faith, the ceremony of washing the deceased before the burial; serves as a ritual purification or cleansing of the body; should be performed by the *Chevra Kaddisha*

Tallith: prayer shawl worn by men during the Morning Prayer service in the Jewish faith

Tehillim: in the Jewish faith, prayers said before the funeral by a group of friends and the shomer; taken from the book of Psalms

Temple: religious building of the Reform and Conservative Jewish faith

Torah: book of law, instruction, and learning

Yahrzeit: (*Mahzeit*) in the Jewish faith, anniversary of a death

Yarmulke (Kippah, Yamaka): in the Jewish faith, skullcap worn by the men at temple services and funeral services

Yizkor: in the Jewish faith, memorial service recited four times a year

Other, Related Terms

ALAR HASHALOM: phrase used after the name of a departed male, meaning *Peace be upon him.*

ALEHAW HASHALOM: phrase used after the name of a departed female, meaning *Peace be upon her.*

ARK: focal point of service in a synagogue or temple; receptacle of the Torah (written law); may be portable or an opening in a wall

AVELIM: mourner; nearest of seven blood relatives – father, mother, husband, wife, child, brother, sister; (*Able, Avel, Ovel*)

BAIS HAKEVOROUS: burial grounds

BAR MINEN: deceased male

BAT MINEN: deceased female

BET OLAN: to bury; everlasting home, graveyard, or burial grounds; (*Bais Olam, Bet Almin*)

BIMAH: portion of the synagogue or temple raised above the congregation seating

DAVEN: to pray

ETERNAL LIGHT: traditionally an oil lamp

GILGUL HANEFESH: transmigration of the soul

KABBALA: tradition

KEVER: grave

MAKOM: place of burial

MINYAN: quorum of ten men over the age of thirteen

MUSOF: prayers

NER TAMID: traditional oil lamp

NIFTAR: deceased

OLAM HABA: the world to come

PHO NIKBAR: monument inscription

SEUDAT: meal of consolation

SHIVAH CANDLE: special candle burned during the seven days of mourning

SHALOM: word of many meanings: *good morning, peace, hello, good-bye, love, until tomorrow, farewell*

SOUL: source of life (*Nefesh, Neshamah, Rucah*)

TEHIYYATH HAMATHEM: resurrection of the dead

TOMB: general term designating places suitable for reception of a dead human body

UNVEILING: tombstone consecration; usually done one year and one day (following the Hebrew calendar) following death

YARHZEIT CANDLE: candle burned for twenty-four hours on the anniversary of a death

Chapter 6 Review

1. Describe the hashkava.
2. What is the role of the chevra kadisha?
3. Describe the burial garments for males and females.
4. Review special requirements for notification of clergy, removal of remains, preparation of remains, and dressing and casketing for each group included in this chapter.
5. Define the following terms:
    a. Taharah
    b. Aron
    c. Shomer
    d. Levaya
    e. Shiva
    f. Sholoshim
    g. Yahrzeit

Chapter 7
The Islamic Funeral Rite

The Islamic Funeral Rite

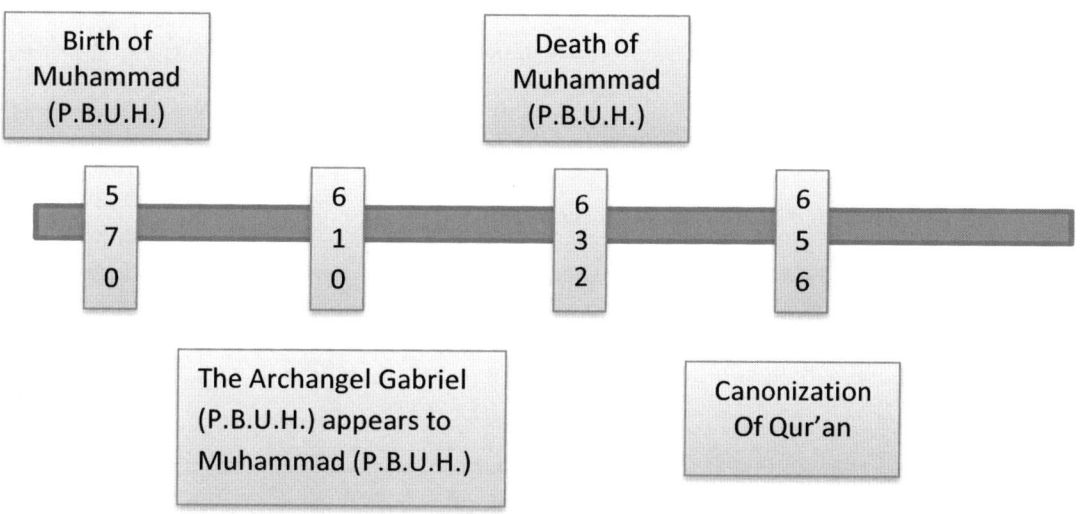

Introduction

The Islamic faith traces its origin back to Adam, the first prophet of Islam (Qur'an Al-Maa'idah 5:3). The last prophet Muhammad (P.B.U.H.) was given the instructions of Islam through the archangel Gabriel (P.B.U.H.). These verbal instructions were compiled by his friends shortly after his death. Today these instructions are known as the Qur'an. Islam is a monotheistic faith which exalts "Allah" as the one true God.

> **Fun Fact**
>
> The first mosque in the United States was constructed in Ross, North Dakota, 1929-1970.
>
> The "Mother Mosque of America" was built in 1934 (Cedar Rapids, Iowa) and is the oldest standing mosque in the United States.

Notification of Death

There are no religious tenants that require the funeral professional to notify the Imam or Mosque at the time of death. In cases of lingering illness, the family is encouraged to be with the dying, to encourage repentance, and the recitation of the *Shahada* ("There is no God but Allah."). For those deaths which occur at home, the family is encouraged to close the eyes, bind the lower jaw, and cover the deceased with a clean sheet.

Removal of Remains

Civil law will determine if there are any restrictions regarding removal. It should be noted that adherents to Islam do not believe in autopsies. However, this is one area where civil law supersedes religious beliefs.

Preparation of the Remains

Common practice is for burial to take place as quickly as possible. This does not mean the burial has to take place within twenty-four hours, or that burial cannot be postponed until family and friends have time to arrive. Embalming is prohibited, however, unless required by civil law, and cremation is strictly forbidden.

The primary preparation of the deceased will be the *Al-Ghusl* (*Ghusl*), or ceremonial washing of the deceased. This washing should be done in a private place where members of the faith community can perform this rite. Warm water, soap, and lotus leaves or camphor should be available, or will be provided by those who perform this task. This washing is done at least three times, and may be performed above this any odd number of times. Men will wash men, and women will wash women. It is permissible for husbands and wives to perform the Ghsul for their spouse or their children.

Dressing and Casketing

After the washing of the deceased, the team will then shroud the deceased in the *Kafan*. The Kafan for a man will

Helpful Terms

Allah: proper name for God in the Islamic faith

Islam: religion which exalts "Allah" as the one true God, and Muhammad (P.B.U.H.) as His prophet

Muslim: name given to a follower of Islam

Imam: spiritual leader of the local mosque

Ghusl: practical and ceremonial washing of a deceased Muslim

Koran (*Qur'an*): holy book of Islam, as revealed by Gabriel to the Prophet Muhammad (P.B.U.H.)

Kafan: burial cloth (garments) utilized by the Islamic community

Qiblah: direction of Mecca, toward which Muslims face during prayers

Janazah: Islamic funeral service and funeral prayer

Mosque: place of worship in the Islamic faith; simple facility designed for prayers and worship, without instruments or seating

> **P.B.U.H.**
>
> This salutation is called the *salawat,* and is translated "Peace be upon him." It is used after mentioning the name of the prophet or of angels. When mentioning names of righteous females, it is translated "Peace be upon her."
>
> This salutation appears in print as P.B.U.H., pbuh or *saw*. It is utilized in this document out of respect to the Islamic faith.

consist of three white winding sheets, while the Kafan for a female will consist of two winding sheets, a sleeveless shirt, a waist wrapper and a head veil. After the deceased is wrapped in the Kafan, the service should follow as quickly as possible.

Historically, it is preferable for the deceased to be buried only in the Kafan. When a casket is required, the family may choose from available selections of wood, steel, or bronze. Those who casket the deceased will make sure to turn the head so that upon burial it will be facing *Qiblah*. In some areas the deceased is placed on his or her right side in the casket.

Pre-Service Considerations

Since the body will be shrouded, there is no viewing or other pre-service.

The Funeral Service

The funeral service is called the *Janazah*. It is a divine service held for every Muslim. The service is usually held outside the Mosque or the *Musalla* (prayer room). The body of a female Muslim is positioned parallel to the wall with her midpoint at the precise location marking Qiblah. Males are positioned the same way with their heads at the location marking Qiblah.

The Imam will stand closest to the deceased facing Qiblah and will lead the Janazah. The service is one of faith and respect. It is considered extremely disrespectful for loud mourning or wailing to

accompany any aspect of the service.

The Committal Service

It is recommended that adherents be buried in Muslim cemeteries. In areas where burial is permitted with the Kafan, the grave must be dug in such a way that the deceased is positioned on their right side facing Qiblah. The grave is dug with a hollowed out chamber. The deceased is positioned facing Mecca, and dirt is used to prevent the deceased from falling back as the grave is filled. It is customary for only the men to attend the graveside service.

Since most burials in the United States will utilize a casket, the positioning of the body will already be secured in the casket. The interment will ensure that the individual is facing the proper direction upon burial.

Rules of Mourning

The Islamic faith community recognizes that grief and its expression are inevitable. The mourner is permitted to grieve, just not in a manner that is offensive to the faith. The mourning periods are stated in the Qur'an. The mourning period should be for three days, except for widows who are permitted to mourn for "four months and ten days."

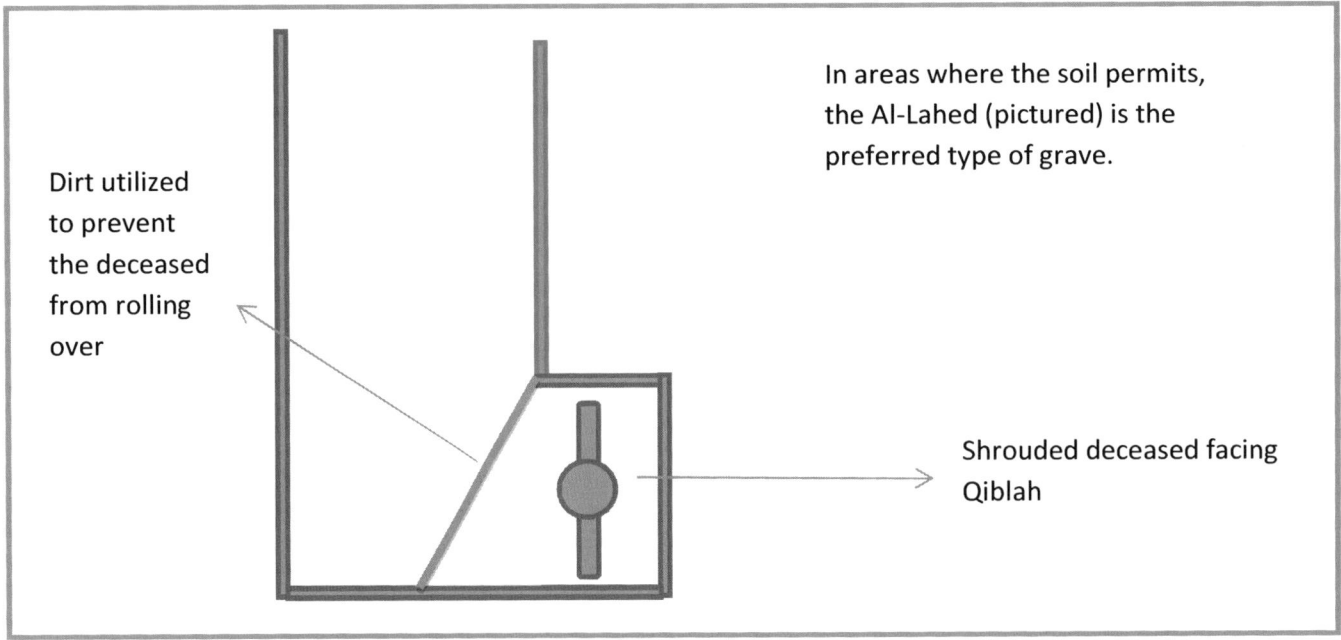

The Stationing in the Mosque or Musulla for the Janazah

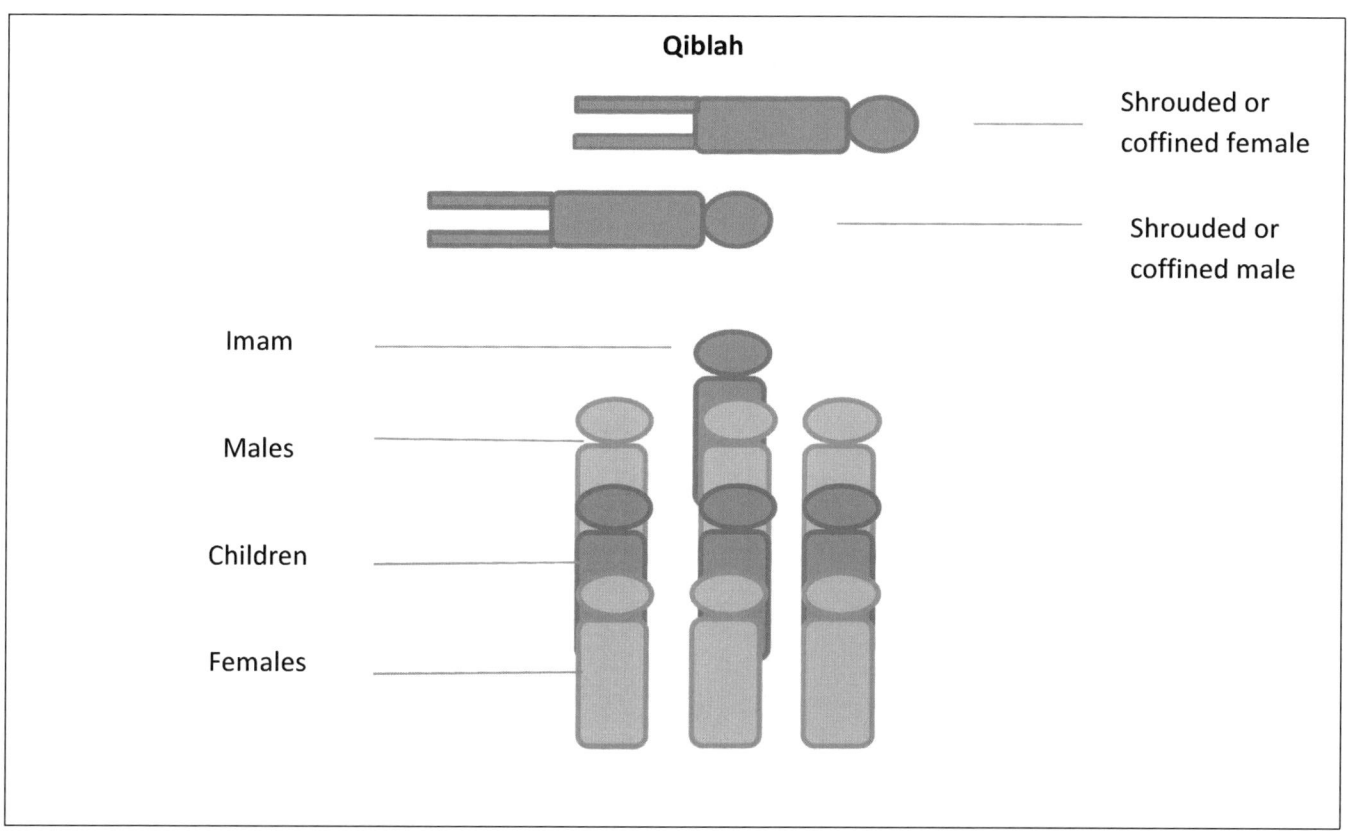

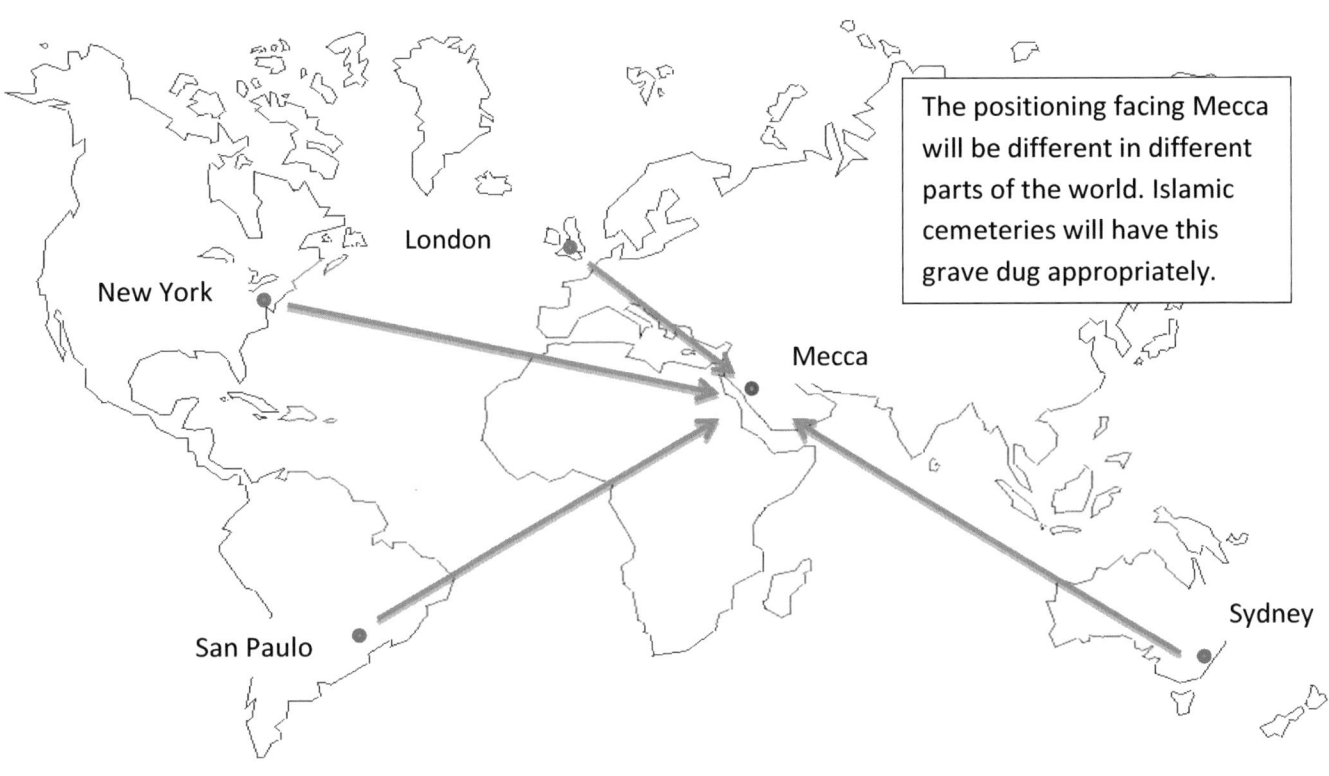

Information Topics	General Information
Classification	Islamic
Origin	Mohammed
Text	Koran
Officiant	Imam
Clergy Notification	not required
Removal	no restrictions
Preparation of Remains	Al-Ghusl (Ghusl)
Dressing and Casketing	Kafan
Pre-Service	no viewing
The Funeral Service	Janazah
Place of Service	outside mosque or musalla
Processional	none
Rubric	none
The Committal Service	buried facing Mecca, if possible
Rules for Mourning	widows – 4 months and 10 days; 3 days for everyone else

Glossary of Islamic Terms

Allah: proper name for God in the Islamic faith

Ghsul: practical and ceremonial washing of the deceased Muslim

Imam: spiritual leader of the local mosque

Islam: religion which exalts "Allah" as the one true God and Muhammad (P.B.U.H.) as His prophet

Janazah: Islamic funeral service and funeral prayer

Kafan: burial cloth (garments) utilized by the Islamic community

Koran (Quran): Holy Book of Islam, as revealed by Gabriel the Prophet of Muhammad (P.B.U.H.)

Mohammed (Muhammad): last prophet of Islam

Mosque (Masjid): place of worship in the Islamic faith; simple facility designed for prayers and worship, without instruments or seating

Muslim: name given to a follower of Islam

Qiblah: direction toward Mecca which Muslims face during prayers

Chapter 7 Review

1. What is the Shahada?
2. Who participates in the Ghsul?
3. What is the Islamic view of embalming and cremation?
4. Review special requirements for notification of clergy, removal of remains, preparation of remains, and dressing and casketing for each group included in this chapter.
5. Define the following terms:
    a. Allah
    b. Al-Ghusl (Ghusl)
    c. Janazah
    d. Kafan
    e. Koran
    f. Mosque
    g. Kiblah

Chapter 8: The Buddhist Funeral Rite

The Buddhist Funeral Rite

Related to Vietnamese, Chinese, Korean, and Japanese Cultural Backgrounds

Three Main Religions of the Orient

Buddhism	Confucianism	Taoism
The teaching of Guatama Buddha is that suffering is inherent in life and one can be liberated from it by mental and moral self-purification. The place of worship is a Pagoda.	The teaching of Confucius is related to the path of virtuous conduct, morals, and ethical principles which regulate individuals and society. The place of worship is a Temple.	Taoism is a mystical philosophy, founded by Lao-tzu, teaching the conformity to the TAO by unassertive action and simplicity. The place of worship is a Temple.

Introduction to Buddhism

Buddhism is a non-theistic philosophy based on proper principles of living (*dharma*). It is a holistic belief that encompasses religion, practice, and community. The majority of teachings are based upon the philosopher Siddhartha Gautama, the Buddha or "enlightened one." Since it is based upon conduct rather than dogma, it can easily embrace other philosophical systems, as well as deeply held traditional practices. The goal of Buddhism is to reach *Nirvana*, a state that ends the cycle of death and rebirth. Once this cycle is ended, self-actualization is realized and the needs of the self (ego) are no more. This state can be reached by following "The Noble Eightfold Path."

The funeral rite derives from the principles and practices of Buddha, Confucius, and Lao-tzu, along with traditional ancestral worship. As an example, the *Deceased*

Helpful Terms

Dharma: the right way of living; the holistic order of all things

Nirvana: literally "to blow out"; the ultimate loss of self and unification with all things

Deceased Altar: placed before the casket with photos, candles, oil lamp, incense vase, flowers, fruits and food

Buddha Altar: placed at a right angle to the Deceased Altar; contains an image of Buddha, incense, candles, flowers, and fruits

Paper Joss: money burned to assist the deceased in the afterlife

Altar is related to Confucianism; the *Buddha Altar* is related to Buddhism; and the *Burning of Paper Joss* or votive money is related to Taoism.

General Considerations

The cultural diversity of this faith group means that certain variations may occur with each family. During the funeral arrangement the funeral professional should ask the family about special arrangements regarding a religious funeral. Frequently the family is able to provide necessary information and indicate their specific wishes related to the disposition based on their cultural background. The funeral service is based upon what is best for the entire family and the community. Help may come from uncles, aunts, nephews, etc. The funeral professional will need to maintain close contact with the family in order to be able to assist and coordinate effectively in each step of the funeral.

> **The Three Jewels**
> 1. The Buddha
> 2. Dharma (the teaching)
> 3. Sangha (the community)

Notification of the Pagoda

The family notifies the Pagoda and the *Bonze* (the Buddhist Priest) of their preferences concerning the funeral and disposition. There are no regulations regarding the time at which this notification is to take place.

Removal of and Preparation of the Remains

The removal and preparation of the deceased is left entirely up to the family. Embalming is acceptable. The embalmer should be aware of the fact that the family may wish to put rice, gold, or coins into the mouth of the deceased before the closing of the mouth. Wealthy families may put rice and three (3) pieces of gold and pearls inside the mouth of the deceased. Less affluent families may put

> **Helpful Terms**
>
> *Pagoda*: place of religious activities in Buddhist practice
>
> *Bonze*: title for a Buddhist priest
>
> *Ceremony of Declaration of Death*: time the family gathers for emotional support in the reality of death
>
> *Service of Encasketing*: sacred rite of casketing the body in Buddhist practice
>
> *Book of Dates*: calendar utilized in the Buddhist faith providing the appropriate time for encasketing, services, and final disposition

new or shining coins in the mouth. This practice allows the deceased to have provisions during the first stage of the journey to the next life.

Dressing and Casketing the Remains

The funeral provider will need to have a room or chapel prepared for the *Service of Encasketing*. The deceased will be on a table close to the casket. The family may gather for the Ceremony of Declaration of Death prior to dressing or encasketing. Family members wear white clothes and white headbands or turbans. (The size of the headband will indicate the nearness of kinship, with the nearest of kin wearing the largest headband.) This ceremony permits the expression of emotions and allows for family support.

When the Bonze arrives, he begins the Service of Encasketing with prayers and benediction. The time of casketing is determined using the deceased's date of birth and death and the date of birth of the surviving spouse or sons in accordance with the *Book of Dates*. The time of casketing the deceased is very significant for the survivors who believe that the lack of this observance may cause bad events to befall the family in the future.

Watch (Wake) Service and Visitation

The family or Bonze may ask the funeral professional to provide tables which can be set-up as separate altars. The Deceased Altar is placed before the casket with the deceased's photos, candles, oil lamp, incense vase, flowers, fruits, and other foods (a boiled egg, for example, is put on the top of a bowl of cooked rice). The observance is related to the Confucianist cult of the death (ancestors). The

> **Know Your Community**
>
> It is not unusual for families in these communities to have multiple visitations over several days.
>
> It is also common for Christian families to have a Wake with the elements of the Deceased Altar, and yet have a traditional Christian funeral service. This practice permits the community to participate in the grief process according to customs they understand.

Buddha Altar is usually placed at right angles to the Deceased Altar and contains incense, flowers, candles, and fruits. In some communities these tables may be combined as one and placed on either side of the casket.

After setting up these altars, Watch (Wake) Services may begin. The Bonze strikes wooden bells and says a prayer. There may be several services. Viewing and visitation are held between the religious watch services. During the funeral visitation, each time a visitor comes in and bows or posterns before the Deceased Altar the survivor's spouse or son should represent the deceased and bow or postern before the visitor, indicating a return of respect from the deceased.

Burial Procession and Committal Service

If the deceased is to be interred or entombed, when the day and time prescribed by the Bonze has arrived, the burial procession moves from the funeral home to the cemetery, led by the Bonze. The committal service will be held at the place of interment, cemetery or pagoda. At the graveside, the Bonze says a prayer and gives Final Benediction with holy water and incense. Friends or fraternal organizations may give a eulogy for the deceased at this stage. The funeral professional is to coordinate these activities.

Cremation is encouraged and, should final disposition be by means of cremation, the Committal Service is held prior to cremation at the funeral home.

The Noble Eightfold Path

1. Right View (based on the Four Noble Truths)

   A. All things are temporary and unfulfilling (Dukkha).

   B. Clinging to temporal things continues the cycle of death and rebirth (the Start of Dukkha).

   C. Ceasing these desires will end the cycles of rebirth (the End of Dukkha).

   D. Follow Buddha in self denial, self-control, and meditation.

2. Right Intention

3. Right Speech

4. Right Action

5. Right Livelihood

6. Right Effort

7. Right Mindfulness

8. Right Concentration

Post Burial Services

Post burial services are held at the home or the Pagoda. There are seven of these services – one per week for seven weeks (49 days). This observance is very significant because these services help the deceased's soul to pass and go through the best reincarnation.

Mourning Period

The mourning period depends upon the range of closeness of individuals to the deceased. This may vary from six months to three years. Mourners are expected to refrain from festivities and amusement during this time. When working, mourners may wear a black ribbon on the chest or a black band on the left arm as a sign of mourning.

Order of Service

Tolling of the temple bell

Procession:
- Minister(s)
- Casketbearers
- Funeral Director
- Casket (Head end first)
- Funeral Director

Chanting of sutras before the casket by the officiant

Presentation of Buddhist name:
> A posthumous name is conferred upon the deceased by the minister, signifying that he has begun his new existence in the Nirvana.

Offering of incense:
> Several incense burners with bowls of ground-up incense alongside will be placed before the altar. This is the most significant expression in the Buddhist religion, always followed by a quick recitation of spiritual cleansing of the soul and the transference of one's mortality to Nirvana. The order of the offering begins with the immediate family, followed by other relatives, casketbearers, and finally, the congregation.

Gatha:
> The first two verses of a Buddhist hymn will be sung at this time.

Opening remarks

Eulogy

Sermon

Gatha:
> The last two verses of the hymn will be sung.

Condolence Message:
> A condolence message is read to the family on behalf of the congregation.

Words of Appreciation:
> A representative from the family will speak in response to the condolence message from the congregation. (This is usually a very brief expression of appreciation to the congregation for their presence at the service.)

Recessional:
- Ministers
- Casketbearers
- Funeral Director
- Casket (Foot end first)
- Funeral Director
- Family
- Congregation

The Japanese Buddhist Funeral Rite

Introduction

The Japanese Buddhists differ greatly in custom and tradition from the Indian, Chinese, and Korean Buddhists. Historically, all Buddhism is derived from India, but each country, geographic region, and culture has its own unique translation of the original teachings of the Buddha.

Sects of Buddhism in Japan

The schools of thought and practice listed each have their own unique place in Japanese Buddhist practice. Buddhism varies in practice based upon various Buddhist texts and historical development.

School	Doctrine and Practice
Jodo Shinshu – development of the Japanese Rite; still followed by other Schools of Buddhism	Due to man's corrupt state, no amount of practice can assist one in reaching enlightenment. Enlightenment can only be obtained by the power of *Amitabha* (Celestial) *Buddha*.
Jodo Shu	Similar to Jodo Shinshu, but adds the practice of reciting the *nembutsu* (the name of Amitabha Buddha).
Shingon Shu	By practice of the *Three Jewels* one may obtain enlightenment in the present life, without the necessity of the cycle of death and rebirth. This practice is based on Buddhist teachings from India and China.
Soto Shu	Associated with a monastic life and the practice of meditation without the use of mental aids, this practice permits flow of conscience in meditation. Enlightenment comes through meditation.
Nichiren Shu	This practice requires chanting the *Odaimoku* (Buddha's teaching regarding the universal law of nature), based upon the *Object of Devotion*. Enlightenment comes, but is rewarded unconsciously.

> **Helpful Terms**
>
> *Makura-Gyo*: prayer recited at the bedside or prior to the arrangement conference; said or chanted after the death has occurred
>
> *Kasaya*: ceremonial robes worn by Buddhist Priest
>
> *Gatha*: verses of a Buddhist hymn sung during the funeral service
>
> *Words of Appreciation*: message of appreciation from the family given after the funeral service

Beliefs

Buddhists believe that the world is an imperfect place full of suffering and sorrow. The only way to end the suffering is to be released from all physical constraints and become enlightened. All sects pay homage to the Buddha, a mortal being who became enlightened while still on this earth. They believe that the soul joins and becomes a Buddha in Nirvana, the Pure Land. There is no heaven or hell, just Nirvana. Through present practice, or death and rebirth, eventually all will become enlightened and exist forever in Eternal Bliss.

Before Death

Family members will be with the dying as a means of comfort and support. A statue of Buddha may be placed near the dying, and family members in some areas recite verses. There are no official sacraments or prayers given to someone who is dying.

Notification of the Minister

The minister may or may not be notified, depending on the wishes of the family. Traditionally, the *makura-gyo*, or bedside prayer, is to be performed by the minister before the body is moved from the place of death. When this is not possible the makura-gyo is said prior to funeral arrangements.

Removal of the Remains

There are usually no restrictions on moving the body once the mortuary is notified. If the Bonze is present, the body must remain untouched until after the makura-gyo is completed.

Funeral Arrangements

If the makura-gyo was not spoken after the death, the Bonze may recite this prior to the arrangement conference. In many locations the priest will stay to assist the family with planning of the service.

Dressing and Casketing the Remains

There are no specific guidelines for casket and clothing selection for laymen. Clothing will be determined by the family. In some communities other garments will be brought to be placed in the casket prior to burial or cremation. Buddhist priests will usually be dressed in their ceremonial robes, or *Kasaya*.

Pre-service Considerations

Flowers and Japanese confectionery may be placed on the altar for the funeral entirely at the discretion of the family and the minister. Visitations are usually scheduled before the funeral whenever the mortuary can accommodate the family. The minister need not be present for the visitation.

The Funeral Service

There are no restrictions as to the time and place of the funeral service, but it may be held at night so that relatives and friends do not have to take off from work. The casket is placed parallel to the altar and remains open for the entire service, unless otherwise requested by the family. The decision to open the casket or not is left entirely up to the family.

Final Disposition

There are no restrictions or recommendations in regards to disposition. If burial is chosen, a graveside service will be held with the minister present. If cremation is chosen, there will be a cremation service held either at the crematory or in the chapel of the mortuary with the minister present. After the services are completed, the family will return to the temple for a final service to provide closure for the family.

Basic Objectives of Funeral Service Personnel
Objective 6

"Flexibility and Adaptation to Cultures and Customs"

The funeral service professional must develop the unique ability to hide in plain sight. Bringing attention to oneself is a distraction to the family and guests, and in some cases it is considered disrespect to the deceased. The list of potential *faux pas* is endless, and sadly, most of these lessons are learned the hard way. Consider the following.

Removing Shoes:

Some Christian Orthodox and Asian Communities may require the funeral service personnel to remove their shoes either at the home or at the religious facility. Be prepared for this eventuality so as not to cause a disruption.

Sign of the Cross:

It is proper for a funeral professional to make the sign of the cross during Roman Catholic or other liturgical services. Not participating brings unwarranted attention.

Bowing toward the Tabernacle:

In the Roman Catholic Culture, it is common when entering the facility to bow toward the Tabernacle when crossing into the Nave.

Touch:

In many Middle-Eastern communities it is forbidden for a man to touch a woman. However it is common for the men of this community to kiss on the cheek or hold hands when involved in conversation. Yes, this may occur during the arrangement conference.

Take a breath:

Most communities will be forgiving if they believe that the social blunder was made out of ignorance rather than malice. Your willingness to apologize when necessary, and work to recover their good will, will say volumes about your firm.

Memorial Services

Memorial services are held periodically to ensure the deceased's safe passage to Nirvana. More practically, these services give survivors a chance to join each other in fellowship and progress through the mourning period, and thereafter pay homage to and remember the deceased person. The services are scheduled as follows:

7th day after death	17th year anniversary of death
49th day after death	23rd year anniversary of death
1st year anniversary of death	25th year anniversary of death
3rd year anniversary of death	50th year anniversary of death
7th year anniversary of death	Every 50th year thereafter
13th year anniversary of death	

NOTE: *Soka Gakkal*, formerly known as Nichiren Shoshu or NSA, is gaining a large following in the Unites States. This radical new branch of neo-Buddhism does not follow the more traditional styles mentioned above. There is no ordained minister; rather, all services are under the supervision of leaders of each group. Although there is a set ritual to follow for funerals, each leader will impose his own interpretation and whims upon his followers, making the service of each group unique. The funeral professional should check with the leader of each group to determine their specific wishes.

In A Nutshell	
Classification	Buddhist (Traditional)
Origin	Siddhartha Gautama
Officiant	Bonze
Clergy Notification	not required
	family or Bonze say Makura-gyo
Removal	no restrictions
Preparation of Remains	no restrictions
Dressing and Casketing	Ceremony of the Declaration of Death; Encasketing Ceremony based on the Book of Dates
Visitation	Deceased Altar; Buddha Altar; flowers encouraged
The Funeral Service	procession
	incense
	gatha
	opening remarks
	eulory
	sermon
	gatha
	condolence message
	words of appreciation
	recessional
Disposition	burial or cremation

The Buddhist Glossary

Bonze: title for a Buddhist priest

Book of Dates: calendar utilized in the Buddhist faith providing the appropriate time for encasketing, services, and final disposition

Buddha Altar: placed at a right angle to the Deceased Altar; contains an image of Buddha, incense, candles, flowers, and fruits

Ceremony Of The Declaration Of Death: a time the family gathers for emotional support in the reality of death

Dharma: the right way of living; the holistic order of all things

Deceased Altar: placed before the casket with photos, candles, oil lamp, incense vase, flowers, fruits, and food

Gatha: the verses of a Buddhist hymn sung during the funeral service

Kasaya: ceremonial robes worn by Buddhist Priest

Makura-Gyo: a prayer recited at the bedside or prior to the arrangement conference; said or chanted after the death has occurred

Nirvana: literally "to blow out"; the ultimate loss of self and unification with all things

Pagoda: place of religious activities in Buddhist practice

Paper Joss: money burned to assist the deceased in the afterlife

Service Of Encasketing: a sacred rite of casketing the body in Buddhist practice

Words Of Appreciation: a message of appreciation from the family given after the funeral service

Chapter 8 Review

1. Describe the Buddha Altar.
2. Describe the Deceased Altar.
3. Describe the various mourning periods.
4. Review special requirements for notification of clergy, removal of remains, preparation of remains, and dressing and casketing for each group included in this chapter.
5. Define the following terms:
    a. Pagoda
    b. Bonze
    c. Ceremony of Declaration of Death
    d. Service of Encasketing
    e. Book of Dates

Chapter 9 The Bahá'í Funeral Rite

The Bahá'í Funeral Rite

Introduction

The Bahá'í faith is one of the newest and fastest growing groups in the world today. The faith has its roots in Islam. However, it is a faith of inclusion rather than exclusion. It sees God's revelation in all faith practices and believes that each messenger (Abraham, Moses, Buddha, Zoroaster, Jesus, and Muhammad) has given mankind a glimpse into the Divine will and purpose. Just as John the Baptist paved the way for Jesus in Christian tradition, the *Bab*, or Gate (1819-1850), was the first to promote the coming of the *Baha'u'llah* (Glory of God) to the modern world.

Mirza Husayn-Ali Nuri was born in Tehran in 1817 and died in 1892. He became the prophet of Babism and founded the Bahá'í faith. Much of the Bahá'í practice and doctrine is based upon the writings of the Bab. As the promised Baha'u'llah, Ali Nuri actively pursued the teachings of the Bab. His area of influence included modern day Iran, Iraq, Syria, Turkey, Israel, Lebanon, and Jordan. Aside

> **Basic Tenets**
>
> 1. Abandonment of all forms of prejudice
> 2. Full equality of women
> 3. Unity and relativity of all religious truth
> 4. Elimination of extremes in wealth and poverty
> 5. Universal education
> 6. Personal responsibility to search for truth
> 7. Global Commonwealth of Nations
> 8. True religion is in harmony with reason and scientific knowledge.
>
> http://info.bahai.org/bahaullah-basic-teachings.html

from his journeys, he also wrote letters to political and religious leaders throughout the world. Upon Baha'u'llah's death, his son Abdu'l-Baha was able to continue the work, eventually bringing the faith to the West and speaking throughout the United States and Canada in 1912.

Today the Bahá'í faith has its headquarters (the Universal House of Justice) in Haifa, Israel on the slopes of Mt. Carmel. It is headed by nine adult members of the faith who are elected by secret ballot every five years.

Background

> **Fun Fact**
>
> The oldest Baha'i House of Worship is located in Wilmette, Illinois.

The Bahá'í funeral rite will have similarities to the Jewish and Islamic funeral rites. There are some minor variations, but the faith follows Abrahamic religious traditions. The majority of this section is based on *Funerals and Burials, Preparation for: Some practical notes;* Mary K. Radpour (http://bahai-library.com/compilation_preparation_funerals_burials, January 24, 2015).

Notification of Death

Unlike many religious groups, there are no formal clergy involved in the burial process. The family will contact the local community of faith and inform them of the death.

Removal of Remains

It is customary for the body to be washed prior to being removed to the funeral home. If this is not possible, the faith community may wish to wash the body, or permit the funeral home to do so.

Preparation of Remains

The washing of the body is considered a great honor and is usually done by a loving family member.

Nothing is to enhance or delay the decomposition process. Therefore embalming and cremation are forbidden to be practiced, unless mandated by law. The faith does allow its members to donate their bodies or organs for medical purposes. It is suggested that any portion that is used for medical research be properly buried according to Bahá'í faith rather than cremated, as is customary.

Dressing and Casketing

After washing, the deceased is to be clothed in a shroud of either silk or cotton. "The shroud is a piece of cloth approximately seven yards or meters in length, when used for a person of normal height and weight, it can be wrapped around the body in one piece, though this is more difficult than to cut it into four one yard or meter pieces, with each one used for the feet and legs, trunk, shoulders, and head, with the longer three foot piece wrapped the length of the body to hold the other pieces in

Baha'i Ring Inscription

"I came forth from God, and return unto Him, detached from all save Him, holding fast to His Name, the Merciful, the Compassionate."

place. It is not necessary to cover the face, but the shroud may be wrapped over the top of the head, as a shawl" (Radpour).

Those 15 and older will be adorned with a Bahá'í burial ring placed on the forefinger. The local assemblies will usually have these rings available.

Hardwood caskets are required for burial. Metal and softwood caskets are discouraged.

Pre-Service Considerations

According to the Baha'u'llah, "the sooner the burial taketh, the more fitting and preferable." In some communities this occurs within 24 hours. The deceased should not be buried more than an hour's journey from the place of death. This stipulation covers all modes of transportation and is generally marked from the limits of the city.

Funeral Service and Burial

The services will usually occur at the gravesite. The only requirement is the recitation of the *Prayer for the Dead*. This is done by one individual in a dignified manner. Other prayers may be spoken if desired, but this is the only one required. The service is open to all, and is considered a joyful and honoring rite.

Where permitted, it is preferable that the deceased's body be placed with the feet toward Qiblih, or the Baha'u'llah's resting place. It should be noted that this can be

---

Prayer for the Dead

O my God! This is Thy servant and the son of Thy servant who hath believed in Thee and in Thy signs, and set his face towards Thee, wholly detached from all except Thee. Thou art, verily, of those who show mercy the most merciful.

Deal with him, O Thou Who forgivest the sins of men and concealest their faults, as beseemeth the heaven of Thy bounty and the ocean of Thy grace. Grant him admission within the precincts of Thy transcendent mercy that was before the foundation of earth and heaven. There is no God but Thee, the Ever-Forgiving, the Most Generous.

Let him, then, repeat six times the greeting "Alláh-u-Abhá," and then repeat nineteen times each of the following verses:

We all, verily, worship God.
We all, verily, bow down before God.
We all, verily, are devoted unto God.
We all, verily, give praise unto God.
We all, verily, yield thanks unto God.
We all, verily, are patient in God.

accomplished within the Christian notion of being buried facing East. Burial in a Bahá'í cemetery would be preferable, but it is not required. Monuments and markers should also be adorned with the emblem of Bahá'í.

There are no specific times of mourning prescribed by the Bahá'í faith. Bahá'ís are permitted to hold memorial services as they choose.

In A Nutshell	
Classification	Bahá'í (traditional)
Origin	The Bab Baha'u'llah
Officiant	none
Clergy Notification	not required
Removal	washing prior to removal if permitted
Preparation of Remains	no cremation or embalming; donation permitted
Dressing and Casketing	shroud of silk or cotton, burial ring, hardwood casket
The Funeral Service	at the gravesite; within one hour journey from place of death; burial in a timely manner; prayer for the dead; feet toward qiblih
Disposition	burial nine pointed star emblem

Chapter 9 Review

1. Which funeral rites are similar to Bahá'í?
2. Describe the shroud used by the Bahá'í.
3. What is the time limit for burial?
4. Review special requirements for notification of clergy, removal of remains, preparation of remains, and dressing and casketing for each group included in this chapter.
5. Define the following terms:
    a. Prayer of the Dead
    b. Burial Ring

Chapter 10
Funerals and the U.S. Military Branches

Funerals and the U.S. Military Branches

Introduction

The United States Government provides a number of services, both financial as well as physical, for the care and disposition of the remains of members of the Armed Forces, both active and reserve, who die while on active duty. Military authorities representing the branch of service the deceased belongs to will assist the family in making the necessary service arrangements.

Services for Active Duty Personnel

Services provided by the government, regardless of which branch of service the deceased belonged to, will include the preparation of the remains, dressing and casketing the remains, transporting the remains (including an escort), and providing a United States flag for the funeral service and disposition.

In many cases the military authorities will make arrangements with a funeral firm holding the United States Government's contract in that area. If the family prefers, they may also choose to make their own arrangements. Up-to-date information on current burial benefits can be found at http://www.cem.va.gov/burial_benefits and also at http://benefits.va.gov/compensation/claims-special-burial.asp.

In addition, families are entitled to the Gold Star Lapel Button for those who lost their lives in armed conflict. "The law provides that one Gold Star Lapel Button will be furnished, without cost, to the widow or widower and to each of the parents and the next of kin" (*The Military Advantage*, 2014 Edition, Terry Howell, page 174). Application form DD3 is used for this honor.

Services for Veterans

Unlike active duty deaths, the funeral professional will have the major responsibility of assisting the family in assuring that all benefits are provided to the veteran's family. The Congressional Research Service defines "veteran" as a "person who served in the active military, naval, or air service, and who was discharged or released therefrom under conditions other than dishonorable." Standard military honors for all branches of military service include the Flag Presentation and the playing of Taps.

The funeral professional will need the deceased's DD-214 to ensure the family has eligibility for services offered by the military. He or she will be responsible for contacting the proper branch of service for honors and/or burial in a National Cemetery, procurement of a burial flag, application for the Presidential Memorial Certificate, and headstone or marker for burial in a private cemetery. The funeral professional should also encourage the family to file for burial and plot benefits to offset expenses incurred.

Helpful Terms

Military Honors: provided at no cost to veterans who have been discharged (other than dishonorably); by law, must include playing of "Taps," the Folding of the Flag, and Presentation of the Flag by a representative of the deceased's branch of service

Taps: a bugle call signaling "lights out" and time to rest; also played at military funeral services

Claim for Standard Government Headstone or Marker (VA 40-1330): application for headstone for burial in a private cemetery, even if privately-purchased headstone or marker is placed

Claim for Government Medallion for Placement in a Private Cemetery (VA 10-1330M): application for medallion for placement on privately-purchased headstone in a private cemetery

The Military Funeral

Regardless of rank, in order for a deceased veteran to have a military funeral, a request must be submitted to the military funeral detail of the branch of service to which the deceased belonged. A military funeral may include both a chapel service and a graveside service, or as is more common, only the committal service at the gravesite.

Military personnel, both active duty and veterans, who are of certain ranks or who have received select military honors may also be eligible

Chapter 10: Funerals and the U.S. Military Branches page 137

for full military honors as part of their funeral service. The funeral cortege for recipients of full military honors includes 21 personnel members. The processional to the graveside will be in this order:

1. Band
2. Escort (including firing party and bugler)
3. Colors and guard
4. Clergy
5. Caisson and casket bearers
6. Honorary casket bearers (if any)
7. Family and friends

Committal Service

If the military portion of the service is to be a graveside service, the military chaplain or the clergy conducts the service. Following the scripture reading and prayers, the firing party (if present) fires a salvo. The bugler plays "Taps" during the folding of the flag, which is then presented to the spouse or next of kin. As the flag is presented, the person presenting the flag will offer the following statement:

"On behalf of the President of the United States, the United States Army (the United States Marine Corps, the United States Navy, or the United States Air Force), and a grateful Nation, please accept this flag as a symbol of our appreciation for your loved one's honorable and faithful service" (Secretary of Defense Memorandum dated April 17, 2012).

According to the same memorandum, members of the United States Coast Guard are welcome to use the same language during the Presentation of the Flag.

Order of Preference for Flag Presentation
1) Widow or widower
2) Children according to age
3) Parents, including adoptive, stepparents and foster parents
4) Brothers or sisters, including brothers or sisters of the half-blood
5) Uncles or aunts
6) Nephews or nieces
7) Cousins, grandparents or close friends

When conducting a funeral for a member of the armed forces, the funeral professional will often find that he or she will be dealing with a multitude of people. This can include the family, the military officials of the Armed Forces branch that the deceased belonged to, and the clergy, celebrant, or officiant. Therefore, the successful funeral professional will work with all involved parties to ensure a smooth process and a service that meets the requirements of all involved.

Helpful Terms

Gold Star Lapel Button: awarded to next of kin for those killed in conflicts with a foreign force

Veteran: "person who served in the active military, naval, or air service, and who was discharged or released therefrom under conditions other than dishonorable" (Congressional Research Service)

Certificate of Release or Discharge from Active Duty (DD 214): official document containing the concise record of military service at the time of separation or discharge from the Armed Forces; necessary for employment, benefits, and re-enlistment

Burial Flag: flag provided at no cost to honor the deceased's service in the Armed Forces; obtained with form VA 2008

Presidential Memorial Certificate (PMC): "an engraved paper certificate, signed by the current President, to honor the memory of honorably discharged veterans who have died" (Howell,Terry: *The Military Advantage, 2014 Edition*, Naval Institute Press, page 175)

Burial Allowance: veteran's benefit allowing family to recover part of the cost of the funeral expense

Plot Allowance: veteran's benefit allowing family to recover part of the cost for burial in a private cemetery

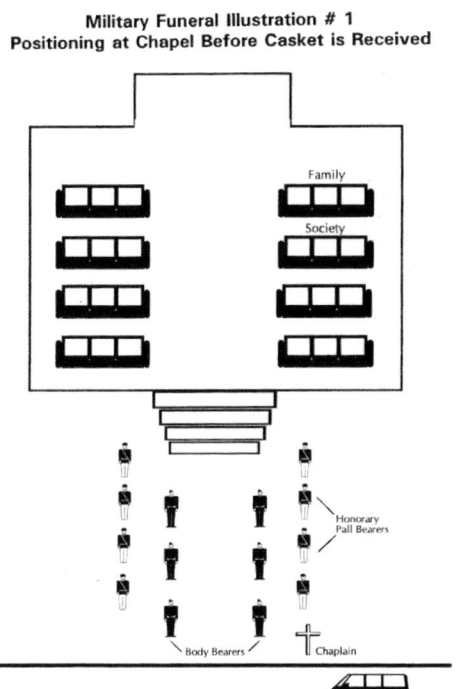
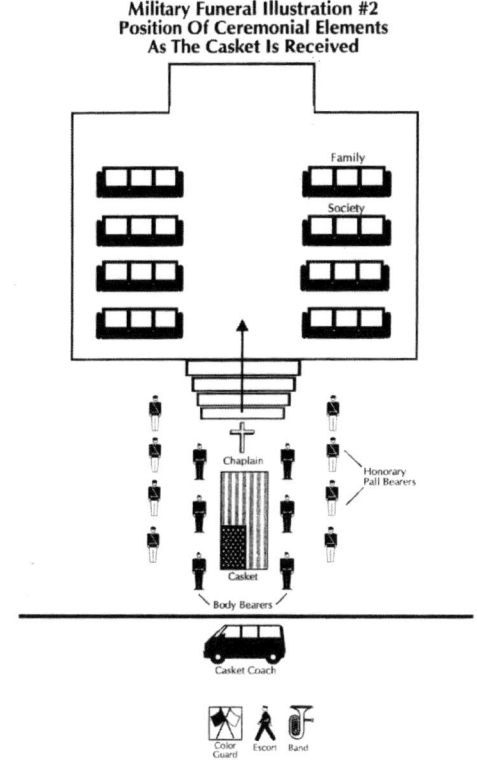
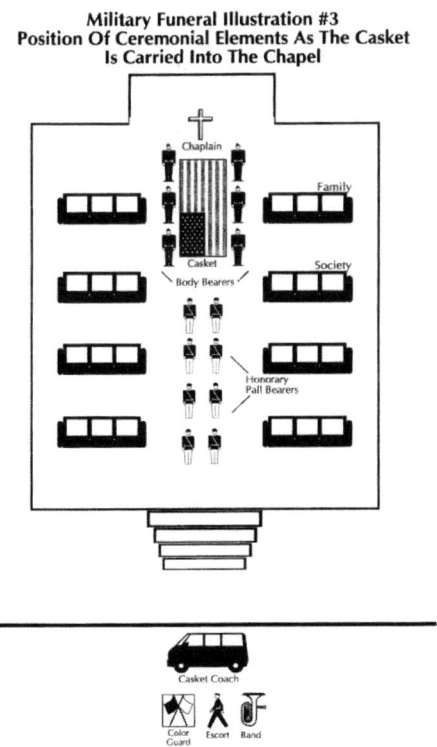
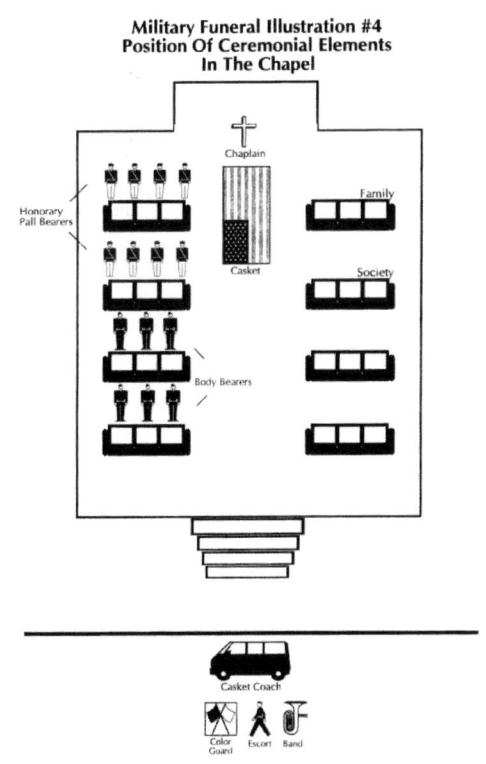

Chapter 10: Funerals and the U.S. Military Branches page 140

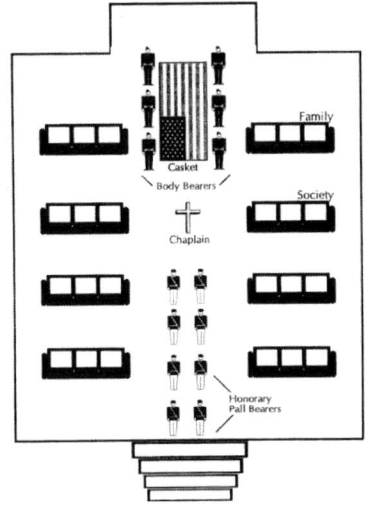
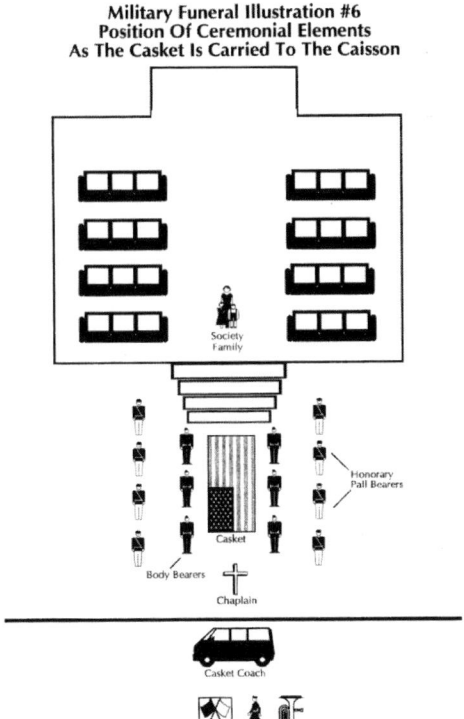
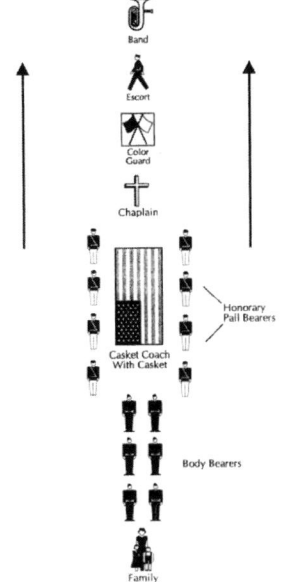
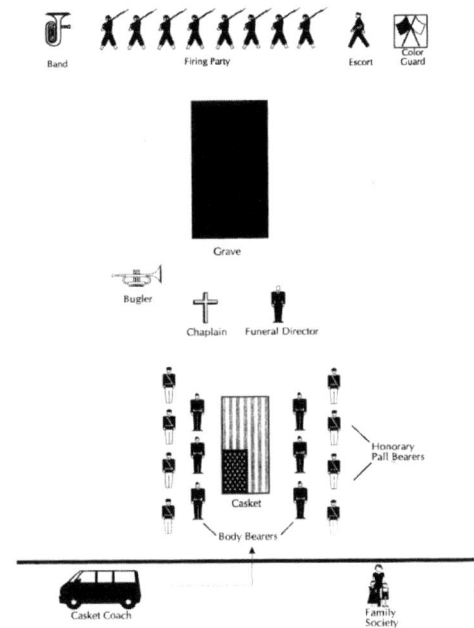

Chapter 10: Funerals and the U.S. Military Branches page 141

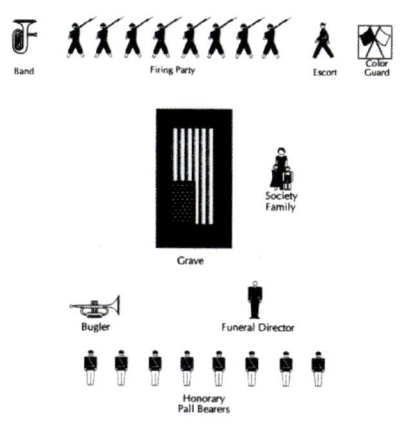

**Military Funeral Illustration #9
Position Of Elements During The
Graveside Committal Service**

Chapter 10: Funerals and the U.S. Military Branches page 142

United States Flag Protocol – Proper Use of the Flag

The United States flag is provided to many deceased Americans to honor their service to their county. The flag which is issued on behalf of the Veterans Administration can be a part of the funeral service in several ways:

1. When used to drape the casket, the flag should be placed as follows:

    (a) *Closed Casket*: Center the flag on the casket so that the blue field (canton) is at the head and over the left shoulder of the deceased.

    (b) *Half Couch Casket*: On an open half couch casket, arrange the flag in three layers (10-inch folds) to cover the closed half of the casket. The blue field (canton) will be the top layer of the deceased's left side. Tuck the white margin along the hoist of the flag under, so that only the blue field (canton) and the stripes show.

    (c) *Full Couch Casket*: Fold the flag into a triangle and place it in the casket cap just above the left shoulder of the deceased.

2. During the military commitment ceremony, the flag which was used to drape the casket should be held waist high over the grave by the casket bearers and folded immediately after the sounding of Taps.

3. Correct method of folding the United States Flag:

    (a) Fold the lower striped section of the flag over the blue field (canton).

    (b) The folded section is then folded over to meet the open edge.

    (c) A triangle fold is then started by bringing the striped corner of the folded side to the open edge.

    (d) The outer point is then turned inward parallel with the open edge to form a second triangle.

(e) Triangle folding is continued until the entire length of the flag is folded in the triangle shape of a cocked hat with only the blue field visible.

4. The flag should not be lowered into the grave or allowed to touch the ground. When taken from the casket, it should be folded immediately.

5. The flag should form a distinctive feature of the ceremony of a statue or monument unveiling, but it should be used as a covering or drape for an item to be unveiled.

6. The flag should never be fastened, displayed, used, or stowed in such a manner as will permit it to be easily torn, soiled, or damaged in any way.

7. The flag should never have placed upon it, nor any part of it, nor attached to it, any mark, insignia, letter, word, figure, design, picture, or drawing of any nature.

8. The flag should never be used as a receptacle for receiving, holding, carrying, or delivering anything.

9. When badly torn, worn, or soiled, the flag should no longer be publicly displayed, but privately destroyed by burning in such a manner as to convey no suggestion of disrespect or irreverence.

10. Nothing should be placed on the flag (such as flowers or a crucifix) when using it to drape the casket.

11. When a flag is transported with the deceased by common carrier, one of two procedures may be followed:

    (a) The flag should be folded and placed in a carton secured inside the shipping receptacle.

    (b) The flag should be draped over the casket when placed in the shipping receptacle.

The Anatomy of The Flag

The United States Flag

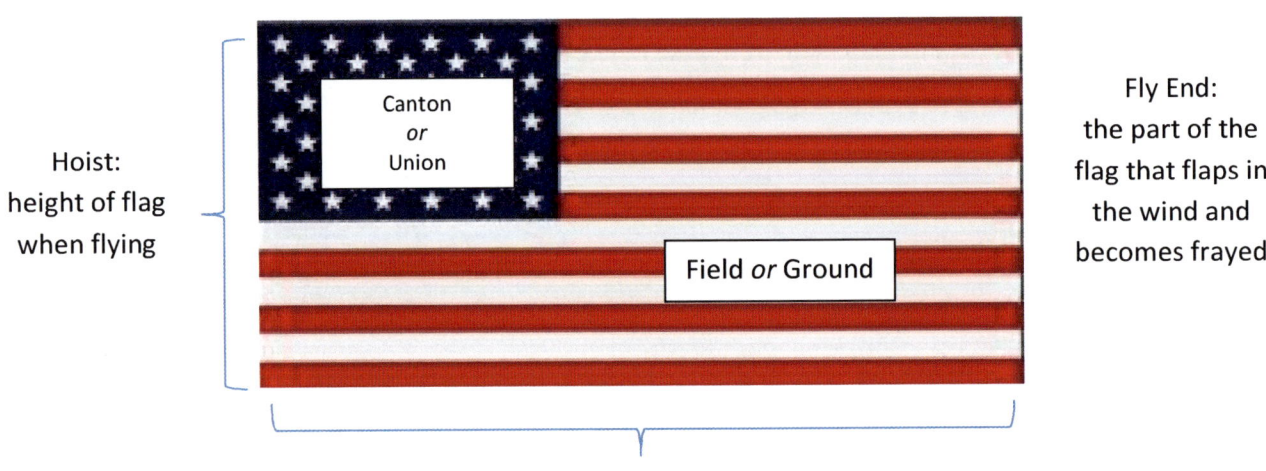

Hoist: height of flag when flying

Fly End: the part of the flag that flaps in the wind and becomes frayed

Fly:
Length (width) of flag; from the end of the canton to the free end of the flag

---

Basic Objectives of Funeral Service Personnel
Objective 7

"Awareness of Honorarium, Policy, and Fees"

Ministers, officiants, singers, instrumentalists, acolytes, and janitorial personnel are worthy of a gift for services performed outside of their normal religious requirements. Each faith group will have different customs in this regard (See: The Church of Jesus Christ of Latter Day Saints). However, a monetary gift is a tangible note of thanks for those providing a service on behalf of the family.

Each firm should be prepared to advise the family on the customary honoraria provided to clergy and facilities in their area. Some organizations may not charge for those who are members, but have a fee for those who are not part of the church (this usually covers janitorial staff). Know the customs of the communities you serve.

It is also good to practice this as a cash advance item. Families may intend to offer a stipend, but amid the grief process forget to do so. Such cases usually put the firm in an awkward situation.

How to Fold The Flag

www.usflag.org/foldflag.html

This custom of special folding is reserved for the United States Flag alone.

How to fold the Flag

Step 1

To properly fold the flag, begin by holding it waist high with another person so that its surface is parallel to the ground.

Step 2

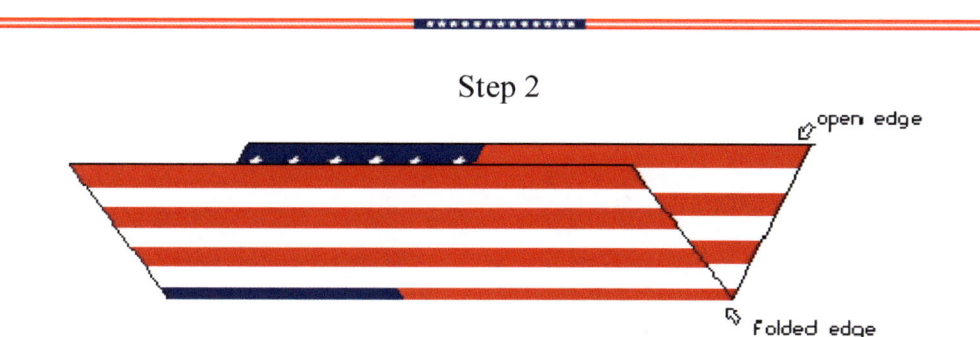

Fold the lower half of the striped section lengthwise **over** the field of stars, holding the bottom and top edges securely.

Step 3

Fold the flag **again** lengthwise with the blue field on the **outside**.

Chapter 10: Funerals and the U.S. Military Branches page 146

Step 4

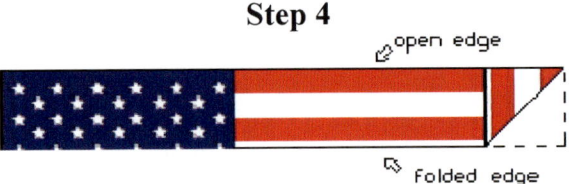

Make a triangular fold by bringing the striped corner of the folded edge to meet the open (top) edge of the flag.

Step 5

Turn the outer (end) point inward, parallel to the open edge, to form a second triangle.

Step 6

The triangular folding is continued until the entire length of the flag is folded in this manner.

Step 7

When the flag is completely folded, only a triangular blue field of stars should be visible.

Fraternal Organizations for the Military

There are a number of veteran's organizations in the United States which also offer their services at the death of a veteran. Perhaps the most widely recognized of these organizations is the American Legion. These groups provide non-sectarian funeral services similar to the military funeral. Services may vary in accordance with the religious beliefs of the deceased. Just as in a strictly military funeral or a funeral containing both religious and fraternal organizations, it is important for the funeral professional to work with all parties involved, including the clergy, post commander, and family, to ensure that everyone understands and is in agreement as to the procedures to be followed.

These organizations provide services similar to those of the military. Unlike the military funeral, which places limitations on the number of military participants, these organizations are able to provide full military honors, including a 21-person funeral detail, or 21-one gun salute. In some cases, there may be as few as three or four individuals to conduct the service. In those instances where a funeral detail of personnel is present for a veteran's organization funeral, the number of individuals and the positions they assume are as follows:

Position	Number Required
Chaplain	1
Bugler	1
Color Bearers	2
Color Guards	2
Commander of the Post	1
Firing Squad	7
Commander of the Firing Squad	1
Casket Bearers	6
Total	**21**

In most cases, the veteran's organization funeral rite takes place at the cemetery. The service may be held in conjunction with a religious committal service or may form the entire committal service. Upon arrival at the cemetery, the chaplain leads the casket (usually covered with a United States flag) front the casket coach to the grave.

The flag is held waist high by members of the particular veteran's organization during the committal service, Taps is played, and the presentation of the flag is made. Often when there are fewer than the 21 veteran members present, the funeral home staff may be called upon to perform some of the functions normally done by the veterans, even including such tasks as the folding of the United States flag and the presentation of the flag to the family. The funeral professional should therefore be fully aware of related protocols should such an eventuality arise.

Many fraternal organizations will have a ceremony to be held either separately or in conjunction with the religious or other funeral service for one of their members. In some cases the fraternal organization will hold its ceremony the evening before the funeral service, much like the Roman Catholic Rosary. In other cases, the ceremony may be held immediately after the funeral service before going to the cemetery. Still other fraternal organizations prefer to hold their ceremony as part of or immediately after the committal service at the cemetery.

It becomes the funeral professional's responsibility to coordinate the participation of the various fraternal organizations in a funeral service. Working on behalf of the family, the funeral professional must remember that each of these participants represents a special and meaningful part of their lives and the deceased's life. As such, they should be accorded the same honor and respect that would be given representatives of the clergy or the military.

	IN A NUTSHELL
	American Legion
History	1919 – present
	Purpose: to advance the aims and interests of veterans, along with continuing the friendships formed during military service
	Leadership: National Commander elected each year at the national convention
Notification of Death	not required; notification regarding participation in funeral service
Making the Removal	no restrictions
Dressing and Casketing	family provides clothing of the American Legion, if desired; no casket requirements
Visitation	military/Ligonier paraphernalia
Funeral	may be traditional religious service with post chaplain participating in or leading the service
Graveside service	21 individuals used in the American Legion service 1. Post Commander 2. Chaplain 3. Bugler 4. Color bearers (2) 5. Color guards (2) 6. Casket bearers (6) 7. Firing Squad (7) 8. Commander of the firing squad
Special Notes	military set-up true of other veterans' organizations
Terms	National Commander Post Commander Post Chaplain

Glossary for the Military Funeral Rite

BURIAL ALLOWANCE: veteran's benefit allowing family to recover part of the cost of the funeral expense

BURIAL FLAG: flag provided at no cost to the honor the deceased's service in the Armed Forces; obtained by form VA 2008

CERTIFICATE OF RELEASE OR DISCHARGE FROM ACTIVE DUTY (DD 214): official document containing the concise record of military service at the time of separation or discharge from the Armed Forces; necessary for employment, benefits, and re-enlistment

CLAIM FOR GOVERNMENT MEDALLION FOR PLACEMENT IN A PRIVATE CEMETERY (VA 10-1330M): application for medallion for placement on privately-purchased headstone in a private cemetery

CLAIM FOR STANDARD GOVERNMENT HEADSTONE OR MARKER (VA 40-1330): application for headstone for burial in a private cemetery, even if privately-purchased headstone or marker is also placed

GOLD STAR LAPEL BUTTON: awarded to next of kin for those killed in conflicts with a foreign force

MILITARY HONORS: provided at no cost to veterans who have been discharged (other than dishonorably); by law, must include the playing of "Taps," the Folding of the Flag, and The Presentation of the Flag by a representative of the deceased's branch of service

PLOT ALLOWANCE: veteran's benefit allowing family to recover part of the cost for burial in a private cemetery

PRESIDENTIAL MEMORIAL CERTIFICATE (PMC): engraved paper certificate, signed by the current President, to honor the memory of honorably discharged veterans who have died (Howell, page 175)

TAPS: a bugle call signaling "lights out" and time to rest; also played at military funeral services

VETERAN: "a person who served in active military, naval, or air service, and who was discharged or released therefrom under conditions other than dishonorable" (Congressional Research Service)

Chapter 10 Review

1. What special benefits are offered to veterans by the military?
2. List the order of the military cortege for services with full military honors.
3. Describe the anatomy of the United States Flag.
4. What is the order of preference for Flag Presentation?
5. Review special requirements for notification of clergy, removal of remains, preparation of remains, and dressing and casketing for each group included in this chapter.
6. Define the following terms:
    a. Veteran
    b. Gold Star Lapel Button
    c. Presidential Memorial Certificate
    d. Military Honors
    e. Taps

Chapter 11
Fraternal Organizations and the Funeral Rite

Fraternal Organizations and the Funeral Rite

It is impossible to identify all of the fraternal organizations which one might encounter in his or her community, or to describe the type of ceremony they might provide for their deceased members. However, a list of some of these organizations and the name of the person who would normally be in charge of coordinating such a ceremony will likely prove to be beneficial in determining the service or services their particular fraternal organization can provide to families in need.

The following chart is provided to assist the funeral provider with a glimpse of organizations that may provide some type of services to these families. Further information may be gained from websites or local chapters.

Fraternal Organizations	
Organization	**Purpose/Composition/Funeral Notes**
Benevolent and Protective Order of the Elks	Began in 1867; "Jolly Corks"; reorganized in 1868 as a civic organization
	Leader: "Exalted Ruler"
	Chaplain: "Worthy Chaplain"
	Provides services suitable for funerals or graveside services
B'nai B'rith International (BBI)	Dates back to 1843
	Jewish humanitarian and human rights organization; fights anti-Semitism
	Offers memorial service prior to regular service
	Appropriate for Orthodox, Conservative, or Reform branches of the Jewish faith
Order of De Molay (Jr. Branch of Free Masons)	Founded in 1919
	Provides leadership skills for boys 12-21
	May offer services at home, funeral home, church, or cemetery
Order of the Eastern Star (Women's Branch of Free Masons)	Composed of female relatives of Masons who hold a Master Mason degree or higher
	Leader: "Worthy Matron"
	Funeral service held the evening prior to service or at the graveside
The National Grange "Order of Patrons of Husbandry" P H (Logo)	Formed in 1867
	Contact Person: Master
	Promotes agricultural regions and issues; "Protect farmers, ranchers and foresters"
	Has its own "Funeral Service" and "Committal Service"; sprig of evergreen placed on casket

Independent Order of Odd Fellows **"To Improve and elevate the character of man."**	First fraternity with mixed sexes as members Originated in England; first US chapter organized 1819 Contact Person: Noble Grand (executive officer) Purpose: "Visit the sick, relieve the distressed, bury the dead and educate the orphans." No national guidelines for funerals Monotheistic organization
Knights of Columbus	Roman Catholic Fraternity Leader: Grand Knight Typically, service conducted evening before Funeral Mass, and often immediately before or after the rosary or Christian prayer service May participate in Funeral Mass
Knights of Pythias	Organized in 1864 Non-sectarian fraternal organization to promote universal peace "Promotes cooperation and friendship between people of good will." Has both funeral service and graveside service at graveside Chancellor Commander at head of casket; Vice-Chancellor and Prelate on each side of foot end of casket (forming a triangle)
Modern Woodmen of America	Founded 1883 Fraternal Benefit Society providing insurance for members Estimated 9 billion dollars in assets in 2009 (not for profit organization) Contact Person: Consul, Master of Ceremonies Ceremony during funeral service and at graveside
Rebekahs	Ladies' arm of the "Odd Fellows" (see above) Contact Person: Noble Grand
Royal Neighbors of America	Fraternal Benefit Society organized in 1888 "By Women, for Women" Contact Person: The Oracle Developed out of Modern Woodmen of America Service led by Oracle; Oracle at head of casket during committal service

The Masonic Funeral Rite

	The Free and Accepted Masons
History	one of the oldest and largest fraternal organizations in the world
	founded in 1717, merging four fraternal lodges; now over 5 million Masons worldwide (estimated 3.5 million in the U.S.)
	monotheistic organization; God referred to as "The Great Architect of the Universe"
	symbols and rituals based on tools and practices of "building" professions
	membership by request, not invitation
Notification of Death	not required
Making the Removal	no restrictions
Dressing and Casketing	clothing provided by family
	Masonic paraphernalia: white lambskin apron and sprig of evergreen for lapel
Visitation	Masonic service sometimes held separately from the religious or public visitation
Funeral	Masonic service after religious portion of service, if in funeral home or secular location
Graveside service	Masonic service at graveside after religious portion of the service, led by Master of the Lodge
Terms	Master of the Lodge

Basic Objectives of Funeral Service Personnel
Objective 8

"Awareness of Local, Regional, and Cultural Variations"

This aspect of funeral service cannot be stressed enough. Faiths that utilize the same rubric will still have cultural traditions which affect the visual aspects and styles of the service. In some Vietnamese Roman Catholic communities, for example, a purple sash is placed over the pall upon entering the nave. Some Chinese Roman Catholic communities bow three times to the deceased after Final Commendation. In one metropolitan area, the family is seated on the Epistle side of the nave, while in the adjoining community the congregation is seated on the Gospel side.

Religious leaders will also make exceptions based on the age of the deceased and mode of death. Liturgical churches have had open caskets during the service, and service styles are often adjusted to meet community needs and requests based on the death event. The traditional service is no longer something the funeral professional can assume. The ability to ask questions, take directions, and adapt during the service is now and will remain paramount.